TILE FLOORS
INSTALLING, MAINTAINING
AND REPAIRING

"It is not good to have zeal without knowledge, nor to be hasty and miss the way."

Proverbs 19:2 (NIV)

TILE FLOORS
INSTALLING, MAINTAINING AND REPAIRING

DAN RAMSEY

TAB BOOKS Inc.
Blue Ridge Summit, PA 17214

FIRST EDITION
FIRST PRINTING

Copyright © 1985 by TAB BOOKS Inc.
Printed in the United States of America

Library of Congress Cataloging in Publication Data

Ramsey, Dan, 1945—
Tile floors—installing, maintaining,
and repairing.

Includes index.
1. Flooring, Tile. I. Title.
TH8541.R36 1985   698′.9   85-17355
ISBN 0-8306-0998-9
ISBN 0-8306-1998-4 (pbk.)

Cover photographs courtesy of Armstrong World Industries.

Contents

Acknowledgments

Like credits at the beginning of a movie, a book should acknowledge those who have participated in its production. Among those who have helped with this book are:

Robert C. de Camara of Armstrong World Industries; Joseph R. Condrill of Azrock Industries, Inc.; Robert J. Kleinhans of and Lis King for the Tile Council of America, Inc.; Louise T. Brennan and Arlene Schueller of American Olean Tile Company, Inc.; Color Tile Supermart, Inc.; E.W. Carls; L.G. Wines; U.S. Department of Agriculture, Forest Service and Extension Service; Department of the Army; Bureau of Naval Personnel; and especially Jim Paterson, Manager of Color Tile Supermart, Vancouver, Washington.

TILE FLOORS
INSTALLING, MAINTAINING
AND REPAIRING

Introduction

Tile floors combine the beauty of ancient and medieval crafts with the employment of modern technology. The skills of artisans can be easily duplicated by the do-it-yourselfer with an understanding of tile floors.

Tile Floors: Installing, Maintaining and Repairing simplifies the installation and maintenance of all types of tiles for both art and function. It will guide you step by step from the design and plan- ning of a tile floor project to the gathering of tiles and tools, the installation of resilient tiles and hard tiles, and proper maintenance of your tile floors. You'll also find practical information on how to re- pair and renovate older tile floors and replace damaged tiles.

Don't let the intricate beauty of tile floors in- timidate you. Learn how to select, install, and care for tile floors with this highly illustrated book.

1

Basic Tile Floors

Floor coverings can add both beauty and function to your home, complementing or contrasting your decor. Floor coverings also say something about their owner: I'm going to be here awhile, or I'm functional by nature, or I've got children.

The term *floor coverings* is used for all of the materials that can be put over a subfloor to provide the finished surface upon which people walk, stand, and carry out a variety of activities. Floor coverings get more use than any other surface in the home. The covering is not only the background for the room decor, but it can help insulate the floor, provide cushioning, and absorb sound. Performance is therefore an important consideration in selection, along with color, pattern, and texture.

Floor coverings can be grouped as *hard, resilient*, and *soft*. Each grouping has different performance characteristics, and there are variations within each group.

Hard floors include slate, brick, concrete, ceramic tile, wood, and some plastic coatings. They don't have any cushioning effect, although some,

such as wood, are less hard than others, such as concrete. They are slippery when wet, and a fall can mean a broken bone. They reflect sounds back into the air. They are however, very durable and useful in certain areas of the home.

By contrast, soft coverings, such as rugs and carpets, provide softness and warmth underfoot, insulate the floor from cold, absorb sound, and are not slippery. These advantages, coupled with the decorative effect, have resulted in the manufacture of carpets for kitchens, bathrooms, laundry rooms, and outside living areas. Man-made fibers and special waterproof backings are combined in constructions that are easy to keep clean and give satisfactory service.

In between the hard and soft floor coverings are those that are termed resilient. They are more comfortable underfoot than the hard floors and vary from a slight resilience to a considerable amount of cushion. Resilient flooring is most popular in areas that need greater cleanliness, such as bathrooms and kitchens.

FLOORING FORMS

Floor coverings, or *flooring*, come in two forms: sheets and tiles. A flooring sheet is usually 2 or more feet wide and 4 or more feet long. In the case of a sheet of carpeting it may be 8 or 12 feet wide × 20 or more feet long. A sheet of linoleum may be 6 × 12 feet or more.

Smaller units are called *tiles*. Hard tile flooring, such as quarry tiles, may be 12 × 12 inches in size or some irregular shape of approximately that size. Asphalt tiles are typically 9 inches square. Ceramic tiles come in 12-inch squares, 6-inch squares, and various odd shapes of these approximate sizes.

This book presents primarily the selection, installation, and maintenance of tile flooring. Some coverage will also be given to sheet flooring to guide you in choosing and installing such flooring, as well as in making comparisons.

RESILIENT TILE

Let's first look at the easiest and most popular type of tile flooring in use today: resilient tile. Figures 1-1 through 1-19 illustrate the various types and styles of resilient flooring, as well as give you some decorating ideas.

Asphalt tile is still available, but has been largely replaced by vinyl asbestos tile. Asphalt tile is low in price, but is harmed by grease, food splatters, and petroleum-based cleaning solutions and waxes. It may soften and stain, has a grainy surface, and is difficult to maintain. It must be waxed regularly. Make sure that the tile you purchase at a "Clearance Sale" isn't asphalt tile.

Linoleum is made of a combination of oxidized linseed oil, resins, wood flour, and coloring material pressed into a felt base. The word "linoleum" should be used only for this product, since it doesn't perform like vinyl floor coverings and requires different care. While it is resistant to grease, it can be harmed by alkalis. Therefore, it cannot be installed on concrete that is in direct contact with the ground because moisture and alkali can move up through the concrete and felt backing into the linoleum. Because alkali materials are used in

powders sold for floor washing, care must be taken to use mild products and leave them on the linoleum only two or three minutes. The surface of linoleum is porous and should be sealed before a wax or liquid floor dressing is applied. Traffic leaves tiny scratches, digs, and scrapes on linoleum so that it may have a worn appearance before its useful life is over. Tips on maintaining linoleum floors will be presented in Chapter 5.

Vinyl-asbestos tile is composed of vinyl resins and asbestos fillers. It is moderate in cost, very durable, and easily cleaned. It can be used over on-grade and below-grade concrete, as well as on suspended wood subfloors. Resistance to alkali and grease is exceptionally good.

Homogeneous vinyl tile is unbacked and usually has uniform composition throughout. It is higher in cost than vinyl-asbestos tile. It can be installed on suspended wood subfloors or over on-grade and below-grade concrete. It is durable and easily cleaned.

Vinyl sheet flooring is available as *inlaid* (the pattern goes throughout the wear layer of vinyl) and as *rotogravure* (the pattern is printed on a sheet that is then covered with a layer of clear vinyl as the wearing surface). The thickness of both types of wear layers varies with the price of the floor covering. Vinyl sheet floor coverings range from having no cushion at all to a thick cushion beneath the wear layer. Special backing material is applied to some vinyl coverings so they can be used on concrete that is in contact with the ground.

No-wax sheet flooring is not a vinyl surface but a new product to which, it is claimed, wax will not stick. If the gloss dulls after several years of service, the manufacturer can provide a special floor finish for periodic application in traffic areas.

SELECTING RESILIENT TILE

There are a number of important factors to consider when selecting from the broad group called resilient floor coverings. They include the gauge or thickness, resilience, underfoot comfort, quietness, light reflectivity, effects of radiant heating, flammability ratings, and relative cost.

The durability of the floor covering depends

Fig. 1-1. Vinyl resilient floor tile (courtesy Azrock Floor Products).

Fig. 1-2. Resilient floor tile in the kitchen and dining area (courtesy Azrock Floor Products).

4

Fig. 1-3. Vinyl resilient no-wax floor tile in the hobby room (courtesy Azrock Floor Products).

Fig. 1-4. Vinyl resilient no-wax floor tile with a soft design for the sewing room (courtesy Azrock Floor Products).

Fig. 1-5. Vinyl resilient no-wax floor tile in the pantry (courtesy Azrock Floor Products).

Fig. 1-6. Vinyl floor tile designed to simulate paver tiles (courtesy Azrock Floor Products).

Fig. 1-7. Vinyl resilient tile designed to simulate quarry tile (courtesy Azrock Floor Products).

Fig. 1-8. Resilient no-wax floor tile simulating wood parquet flooring (courtesy Azrock Floor Products).

Fig. 1-9. Resilient floor tile in a simulated parquet flooring design (courtesy Azrock Floor Products).

Fig. 1-10. Resilient no-wax floor tile in a simulated ceramic tile design (courtesy Azrock Floor Products).

Fig. 1-11. Resilient no-wax floor tile can also simulate patio tiles (courtesy Azrock Floor Products).

Fig. 1-12. This resilient no-wax floor tile is designed to look like ceramic tile (courtesy Azrock Floor Products).

Fig. 1-13. Resilient tile can offer both beauty and easy maintenance to a mud room (courtesy Azrock Floor Products).

Fig. 1-14. Vinyl resilient floor tile simulating a stone tile floor (courtesy Azrock Floor Products).

Fig. 1-15. Resilient tile can even offer the look of glaze to simulate ceramic floor tile (courtesy Armstrong World Industries).

17

Fig. 1-16. Resilient no-wax floor tile with a glazed tile design (courtesy Armstrong World Industries).

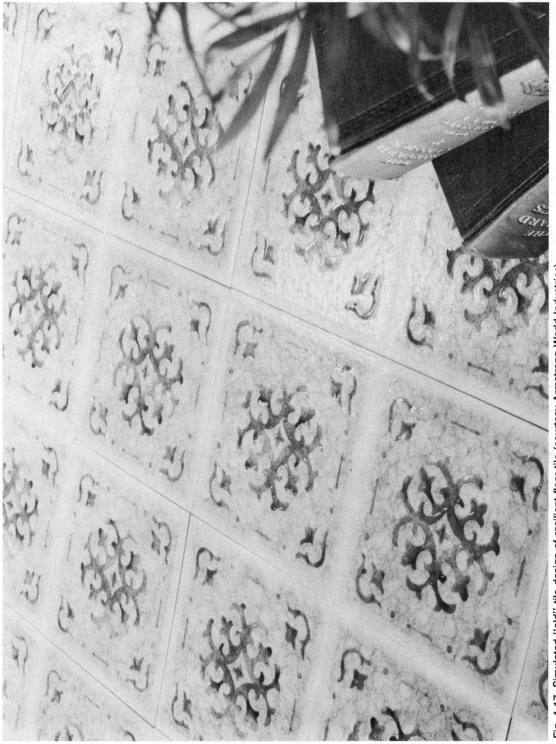

Fig. 1-17. Simulated "old" tile design of resilient floor tile (courtesy Armstrong World Industries).

Fig. 1-18. Resilient tile can also simulate pavers (courtesy Armstrong World Industries).

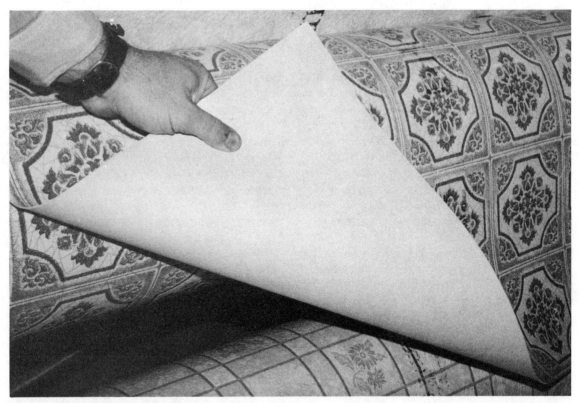

Fig. 1-19. Resilient vinyl sheet flooring.

partly on the thickness of the wear layer. Modern manufacturing methods and improved materials have resulted in durable wear layers that are thinner than formerly needed. The wear layer is either that part containing the color and pattern, or it is a transparent layer above it. Inlaid vinyl and linoleum, remember, have the pattern all the way through the wear layer. Printed vinyl sheet flooring and some of the tiles have a wear layer above the pattern, which varies from 6 mils to several times that thickness. Normally, at least 10 mils is needed to resist damage by sharp objects.

Quietness and comfort vary with the total thickness of the floor covering from the backing to the surface. The thicker floor coverings absorb more impact and are therefore less noisy and, at the same time, provide more cushion for walking and standing. The cushioned floor coverings vary both in thickness and in the amount of cushion provided.

Resilience is the elasticity of a material, which causes it to regain its original shape after being indented. The impact from walking traffic can be several thousand pounds per square inch, especially with tiny heels. It isn't possible to control the indentation that flooring may receive, but the results can be minimized if light, multicolored floorings are chosen in patterns that have swirl, marblelike graining, terrazzo, mosaic, or spatter-dash mottling. Embossed surface textures and low gloss also conceal indentations. To reduce the indentation from heavy furniture, floor protectors of adequate size should be used under furniture legs. Don't use dark protectors, though, because they discolor both vinyl and linoleum.

Underfoot comfort of resilient floor coverings is affected by the subfloor material as well as the composition of the floor covering. On concrete, a cushioned floor covering will help reduce fatigue from walking and standing. The thicker cushions

21

will also provide some insulation from cold floors.

The sound created by the impact of foot traffic is a common source of annoyance. The sound tends to reverberate to adjoining rooms and is most pronounced in the room underneath. Most resilient floor coverings produce less noise than hard floors, but cushioned floor coverings create much less sound than the uncushioned resilient coverings. This cushion is, however, not enough to stop sounds coming through the floor from the room above.

Room noises, as from voices and equipment, are not absorbed by resilient floor coverings as they are by the textured surface of carpeting. The smooth surface of resilient coverings allows the sound to reverberate.

The amount of light that is reflected by the floor covering helps determine how much light is available for seeing. The tints closest to white will reflect the most light, whereas medium and dark colors will absorb a great deal of the daylight or electric light that reaches the floor.

The amount of gloss on the surface of the floor covering has an effect on the appearance of the finished floor. Smooth, shiny flooring materials tend to show up minor irregularities in the subfloor surfaces and, therefore, require more careful subfloor preparation and inspection before installation. Embossed floor coverings soften the light reflection.

Regarding the effects of radiant heating, tests show that there is almost no loss of heating efficiency through the use of resilient flooring materials. No harmful effects on the floor coverings have resulted from their use on radiant heated floors either.

Floor coverings can be tested for flame spread where this is a concern. Currently, a government directive known as the Hill-Burton Regulations is used to test floor coverings for hospital and medical facilities. Information about the rating of a particular floor covering can be obtained from the manufacturer.

RELATIVE COSTS OF RESILIENT FLOORS

Several factors besides the cost per square foot should be considered in assessing the cost of floor coverings. Perhaps the most important is the expense of preparing the subfloor and doing the installation work. The most expensive floor covering may not perform well if the subfloor is not suitable or the adhesive or workmanship is not of good quality. Installers vary in their experience and reliability, as is true with any trade.

Manufacturers of resilient tile and other floor coverings have manuals that specify the kind of subfloor that is needed for each covering. Retail dealers have this information. Also, Chapter 3 will offer information on subflooring requirements. The method of installation may make it possible for a new resilient covering to be placed over an old covering. The advice of the floor covering retailer can be very helpful.

The size and shape of the room may make tile more economical than sheet flooring because of irregularities that require much fitting and loss of material. The width of the room may require more yardage in sheet coverings than would be needed in tile.

Do-it-yourself installation saves a great deal of money where it is feasible. Some floor coverings can be cut and laid without adhesive, using either double-faced tape or adhesive around the edges. Self-adhesive tiles can be laid by an amateur, and some tiles carry a 5-year guarantee for bonding to the subfloor.

EARLY TILE

As you can imagine, resilient tile is a fairly new product in the history of mankind. The earliest tiles used for flooring and walls were hard tiles. The use of glazed tiles dates from about 4,000 B.C.—two milleniums before Moses was given stone tablets. Excavations of structures built previous to this era have revealed tiles much like those of today. Usage of tiles seems to have stemmed from man's earliest experience with the most primitive plastic, common earth. Man learned to mold and sun-dry various types of earth, and from there it was a simple step to discover the advantage of baking with artificial heat. This led to the discovery that certain materials, if heated sufficiently, would melt and form a glaze. Impressed with the hardness of this glaze, as well as the decorative effects possible, builders experimented further, eventually resulting in a finished product comparable to that which we use today.

Some of the more ornate buildings of ancient times had tile work that was even more elaborate than what we now see. Certain mosaics depicting life of bygone civilizations and inscriptions found on tombs and other structures employed bits of tile-glazed surfaces. Somewhat later, the Aztecs and Incas produced styles and designs of their own, most of which were handmade. Even today, Mexican handmade tile is popular in the United States, particularly in Spanish-style homes and churches.

In modern times, manufacturers have developed better processes and materials for glazes, bisques, and installation. What may have required a craftsman now can be accomplished by a do-it-yourselfer. Refractories have been improved until a host of materials are now available. Recently, new kinds of tile were put on the market, including aluminum with baked enamel finish, steel, cement with terra-cotta surface, and plastic tiles. Wood and fiberboard have likewise been coated with lacquer or plastic, available in large scored sheets. Nearly all these are installed using a mastic substance as the adhesive agent. A newer innovation is a method whereby clay tiles are installed over a thin coating of a substance much like white portland cement. This is known as the thin-wall method. It will be covered in Chapter 4.

HARD TILE

There are literally thousands of types and designs of hard tiles available today for installation on floors, walls, and other surfaces. They range from small ceramic chips to large flat stones. Figures 1-20 through 1-32 illustrate hard tiles and design ideas.

There are two general types of ceramic tiles. Perhaps the best known are the 4 1/4- × -4 1/4-inch tiles that are made in three different textures. The high-gloss type is designed for use on walls, ceilings, trim work, and drainboard splashes—in fact everywhere except on floors and steps. Glazed tiles, however, are often made in various other sizes. In the case of ceramic tiles, they may be 1-inch hex-agon, 3/4-inch squares, or numerous rectangular sizes. High-gloss tiles are rarely used on floors.

Another type of glazed tiles, known as *crystal glazed*, is made with a rough and granular texture, which is more or less slipproof. They may be used on floors in any but public buildings and are one of the most popular tile for floors in private homes. They are suitable for use in all situations where a glazed tile is desirable. Two intermediate glazes known as *matte* and *satin matte*, are also available. They are of value in relieving the glare of high-gloss tiles.

The simplest types of tiles are those that are made of some kind of clay, molded in simple hand molds, and baked. In order to make them more decorative, various colored glazes are applied. In making some of the more primitive tiles, the makers were content with plain unglazed pieces. A modern tile of this type is the Spanish patio tile. It is made of terra-cotta, usually thick and of large size. More elaborate types are made in Mexico, where floral patterns in or under the glaze are used. Some ceramic tile must be soaked in water before setting. Thirty minutes to two hours are usually required for saturation. The *bisque*, or main body of these tiles, is made of red, cream, or the more common white clay. White clay of one type is known as *China clay* and is often used in pottery making.

Other ceramic tiles are tiles and of silicon base with little or no clay added, depending on the color desired. They are pressed in hydraulic molds and are either unglazed or glazed. Similar to these, but generally larger, are the quarry tiles that have a larger proportion of terra-cotta or clay, giving a reddish brick color to most of this material. Modern methods of manufacturing can produce chiefly the vitreous type or those that require no soaking.

Ceramic tiles are often unglazed, in which case they are suitable for either floor or wall work. They are ideal for swimming pools, curved surfaces, or wherever small tile is needed.

Encaustic tiles are those that are made of terra-cotta clays of two or more colors, one color forming the bisque into which designs are etched and another color pressed into the depressions comprising the design. The tile surface is then smoothed,

Fig. 1-20. Ceramic mosaic hard tile installed in the kitchen and dining area (courtesy Tile Council of America).

Fig. 1-21. Ceramic mosaic hard tile installed in the entryway (courtesy Tile Council of America).

Fig. 1-22. Light reflects the depth and beauty of ceramic mosaic tile (courtesy Tile Council of America).

Fig. 1-23. Ceramic mosaic tile used in an Early American dining room (courtesy Tile Council of America).

Fig. 1-24. Quarry tile in the entryway (courtesy Tile Council of America).

Fig. 1-25. Quarry tile can also add a decorative dimension to the living room (courtesy Tile Council of America).

Fig. 1-26. Ceramic tile can also be used for more contemporary designs (courtesy Tile Council of America).

Fig. 1-27. Ceramic tile can beautify floors, walls, and even countertops (courtesy Tile Council of America).

Fig. 1-28. Greenhouse additions often use ceramic floor tile (courtesy Tile Council of America).

Fig. 1-29. Ceramic tile in the great room (courtesy Tile Council of America).

Fig. 1-30. Unglazed ceramic tile (courtesy Tile Council of America).

34

Fig. 1-31. Today's ceramic tile comes in an infinite range of sizes, shapes, and colors (courtesy Tile Council of America).

Fig. 1-32. Ceramic tile can be used to develop mosaic designs in your floor (courtesy Tile Council of America).

leaving a sharp contrast of colors.

Sometimes encaustic tiles are glazed, but the majority are unglazed, presenting a surface much like quarry tile. Glazed encaustic tiles are used as stair risers and on walls.

Quarry tiles are made with a silica base and varying amounts of clay. They are first pressed in a hydraulic press, after which they are baked. Because of the excessive quantity of silica and the density of these tiles, they don't absorb water in any appreciable quantity. The texture of broken pieces shows the vitreous or glassy structure.

Quarry tiles are manufactured in assorted sizes and thicknesses and are either glazed or unglazed. Unglazed types lend themselves to floor work, while the glazed kinds are better suited for wall or other vertical situations.

Patio tiles are similar in appearance to quarry tile but are made of terra-cotta or a clay base. They are never glazed and are soaked before setting.

They are used only for floors and patios, their large size eliminating them from small areas.

Pavers are similar to ceramic mosaic tile in composition, but are thicker and larger so they look much like unglazed tile. Like quarry tile and ceramic mosaics, they can be used outdoors.

Hard tiles such as quarry tiles, pavers, and some glazed ceramic tiles are very popular for installation under wood stoves. They must have a good subfloor and be of a strength and thickness that eliminates the chance of breakage.

SELECTING HARD TILES

The selection and purchasing of hard tiles can be pain or joy depending upon how much you know about them before you step into the first flooring store. I'll cover a number of topics and ideas to help you in this selection. In addition, Figs. 1-33 through 1-41 illustrate the retail selection process.

Fig. 1-33. Typical retail floor tile display.

Fig. 1-34. Watch for special prices on flooring, especially in the fall and spring.

Fig. 1-35. Tiles come in a variety of sizes and shapes.

38

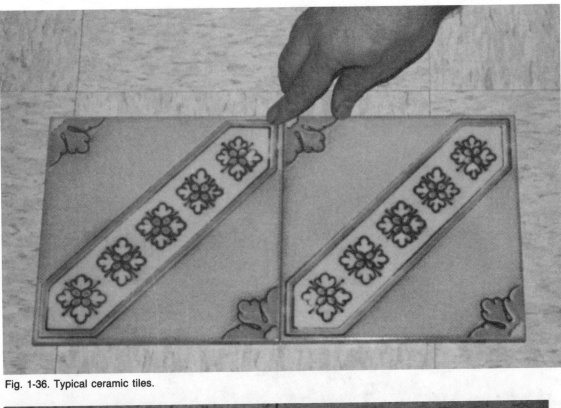

Fig. 1-36. Typical ceramic tiles.

Fig. 1-37. The back side of a ceramic tile designed to allow mastic to adhere.

Fig. 1-38. Display of various ceramic mosaic tile sheets.

First, make sure that the tile you decide upon is suitable for floors. Tiles for floors are generally heavier and thicker than wall tiles, and finishes are either matte or textured. The very high-gloss glazes would obviously scratch underfoot; so they are best reserved for walls.

Color is a matter of taste but it's best to choose conservatively. Because a tile floor is likely to be down for the life of the house, it should be so neutral that it would go with the broadest possible range of furnishing styles and colors.

The neutrals include white, off-whites, tans, grays, and browns. These hues are plentiful in glazed floor tiles as well as in unglazed ceramic

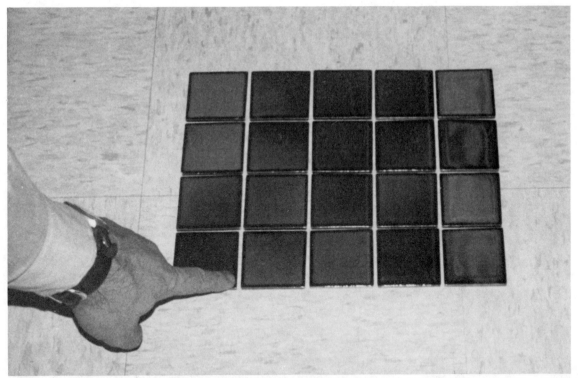

Fig. 1-39. Sheets of ceramic mosaic tiles are uniformly spaced for grouting.

Fig. 1-40. Ceramic tile also comes in sheets with uniform spacing.

Fig. 1-41. Ceramic tile can also be purchased in unique shapes.

mosaics, those tiny 1-inch and 2-inch squares popular in designer homes.

All of the earth tones, which are natural to unglazed quarry tile and pavers, are good neutrals. Until recently, these products came only in terracotta, but they now run the gamut of earth colors from palest sand to darkest umber.

You can use quarry tiles or pavers in any interior except the most formal ones. Pale tiles blend well in contemporary rooms. Warm reddish and brown tones suit colonial and country decors. The darkest colors retain heat extremely well; so they should be used in sun spaces, greenhouses, and other passive solar additions or retrofits.

Choose glazed tiles for formal, traditional rooms. Dark green, burgundy, and gold tones are beautiful choices for interiors featuring fine antiques. Checkerboard designs of black and white tiles are classics for French or Italian period rooms.

Precisely cut, smooth tiles look best in contem-

porary rooms. Tiles with a hand-crafted look, achieved with deliberately uneven edges and random surface textures, are best for traditional and country homes.

Grout, the material that fills the joints between the tile, can help the floor seem more interesting. For graphic impact, choose a grout color that contrasts sharply with the tile. For a monochromatic, quiet effect, choose a grout color to match the tile.

Ceramic mosaics usually come in 1 or 2-inch squares as well as in small rectangles and hexagon shapes. There are glazed and unglazed ceramic mosaic tiles. Generally, only the unglazed tiles should be used for floors. Ceramic mosaics are usually mounted on 1-square-foot sheets with equal grout spacing for easy installation. If you need just a few tiles of the sheet to create a pattern, merely cut the bonding material with ordinary scissors, but don't forget to include the grout line spaces when you lay out loose tiles.

HARD TILE GREENHOUSE

Few homes use hard tiles throughout the house. Rather, they are used selectively in entryways, halls, kitchens, baths, and in add-on greenhouse rooms. In fact, a greenhouse or sun room is an excellent use for hard tiles that capture and release solar energy.

Greenhouses are no longer just for gardeners. Increasingly, they are added onto houses to cut heating bills and, at the same time, add welcome square footage. According to the Tile Council of America, a greenhouse addition can act as a natural solar "collector" and provide appreciable heat gains from the sun. Step-by-step instructions and illustrations for installing such a tile-floored greenhouse are offered in Chapter 4.

The key is a thermal mass that will absorb warmth from the sun and slowly release it as the air cools in the evening or on cloudy days. The thermal mass is usually supplied by a thick concrete slab. Ceramic tile is the only floor covering material that can be used on top of the slab in such solar installations.

Heavy quarry tiles or pavers are great choices for sunspace floors. Dark colors absorb heat better than light ones, so terra-cottas and browns are best choices. Unglazed, natural tile has also been found to absorb heat better than the glazed types.

About 4 inches of floor or wall mass are needed for ceramic tile to serve as a heat sink. It's best to ensure that the heat-absorbing surfaces are not covered with rugs, a lot of furniture, paintings, plants, or other decorations. Masonry planters, tiled to match the floor, and tile-topped counters will soak up the sun's rays, too. Use black water-filled drums as bases for counters or potted tables to increase the room's thermal properties.

Some greenhouse additions harness more sun than they need, and this heat can be used in adjoining rooms. Doors and/or registers can distribute the air. In the summer, awnings or blinds should be used to keep the sun out of the greenhouse. Such shielded tile floors and walls can also help keep the inside cool during the hot months.

Remember that a greenhouse that is supposed to harness the heat of the sun must face the quadrat from the southeast to the southwest. Also consider the trees around the house. Deciduous trees that provide summer shade are usually fine, but make sure that their branches aren't so dense that they block out too much winter sun.

Keep in mind, too, that, in some cases, the addition of a greenhouse to your home will be eligible for a solar energy tax credit. Discuss the requirements with your tax accountant or the Internal Revenue Service.

2

Planning Tile Floors

Once you've selected the type of tile floor you will install, you are ready for the most important task: planning. Good planning is important because it helps guarantee a satisfactory floor, minimizes waste, reduces the number of problems, cuts costs, and makes the job enjoyable. Good planning includes understanding the following: basics of floor construction and covering, how to select and use tiles and tools, how to estimate material requirements, and how to prepare for the job.

BASE FOR RESILIENT FLOORS

Resilient floors should not be installed directly over a board or plank subfloor. Underlayment grade of wood-based panels such as plywood, particleboard, and hardboard is widely used for suspended floor applications (Fig. 2-1).

Plywood or particleboard panels, 4 × 8 feet, in a range of thickness from 3/8 to 3/4 inch, are generally selected for use in new construction. Sheets of untempered hardboard, plywood, or particleboard 4 × 4 feet or larger and of 1/4- or 3/8-inch

thickness are used in remodeling work because of the floor thickness involved. The underlayment grade of particleboard is a standard product and is available from many building material retailers. Manufacturer's instructions should be followed in the care and use of the product. Plywood underlayment is also a common product and is available in interior types, exterior types, and interior types with an interior glue line. The underlayment grade provides for a sanded panel with a C-plugged or better immediately under the face. This construction resists damage to the floor surface from concentrated loads such as chair legs and heavy furniture.

Generally, underlayment panels are separate and installed over structurally adequate subfloors. Combination subfloor underlayment panels of plywood construction find increasing usage. Panels for this dual purpose generally have tongue-and-groove or blocked edges and C-plugged or better faces to provide a smooth, even surface for the resilient floor covering. To prevent nails from showing on the surface of the tile, joists and subfloor

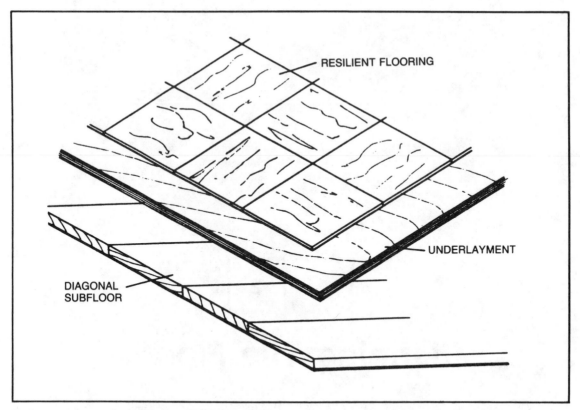

Fig. 2-1. Using underlayment as a resilient floor base.

should have a moisture content near the average value they reach in service.

The thickness of the underlayment will vary somewhat, depending on the floors in adjoining rooms. The installation of tile in a kitchen area, for example, is usually made over a 5/8-inch underlayment when finish floors in the adjoining living or dining areas are 25/32-inch strip flooring (Fig. 2-2).

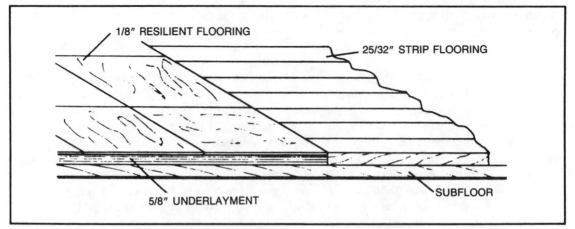

Fig. 2-2. Resilient flooring can also be laid over underlayment to butt strip flooring.

When thinner wood floors are used in adjoining rooms, adjustments are made in the thickness of the underlayment.

Concrete for resilient floors should be prepared with a good vapor barrier installed somewhere between the soil and the finish floor, preferably just under the slab. Concrete should be leveled carefully when a resilient floor is to be used directly on the slab so dips and waves are minimized.

Tile shouldn't be laid on a concrete slab until it has completely dried. One method which may be used to determine this is to place a small square of polyethylene or other low-perm material on the slab overnight. if the underside is dry in the morning, the slab is usually considered dry enough for the installation of tile.

BASE FOR CERAMIC TILE

Ceramic floor tiles can be installed over a variety of bases, including concrete and wood. Figures 2-3 through 2-14 illustrate a variety of suggested installation methods over different bases. The adhesives used will be discussed later in this chapter.

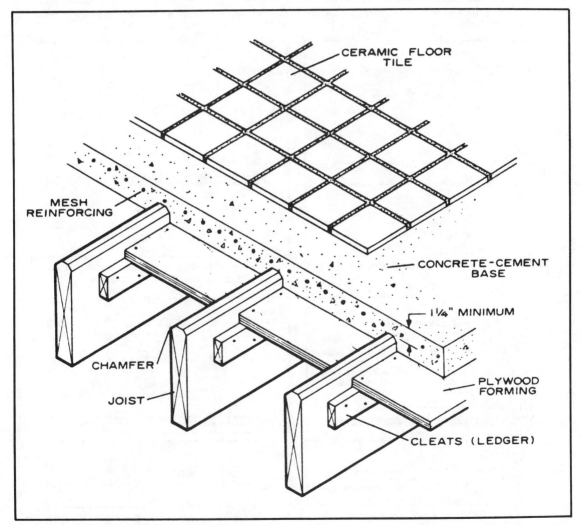

Fig. 2-3. Ceramic tile installed on a cement base.

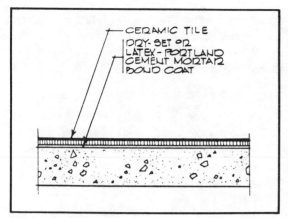

Fig. 2-4. Dry-set mortar over a concrete subfloor (courtesy Tile Council of America).

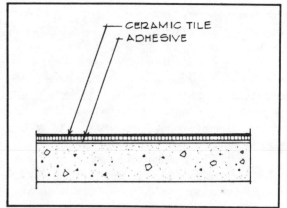

Fig. 2-7. Organic or epoxy adhesive over a concrete slab (courtesy Tile Council of America).

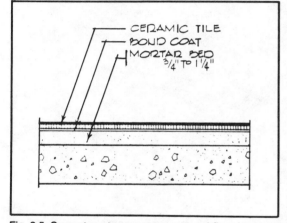

Fig. 2-5. Cement mortar over a concrete subfloor (courtesy Tile Council of America).

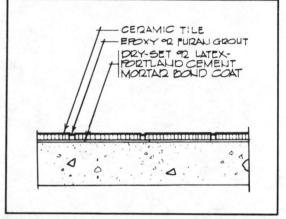

Fig. 2-8. Dry-set mortar and epoxy grout over concrete subfloor (courtesy Tile Council of America).

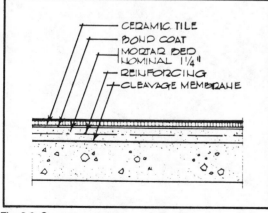

Fig. 2-6. Cement mortar over a reinforced concrete subfloor (courtesy Tile Council of America).

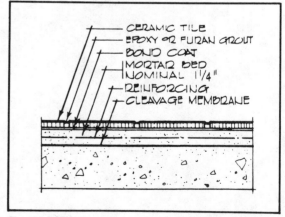

Fig. 2-9. Cement mortar and epoxy grout over concrete subfloor (courtesy Tile Council of America).

48

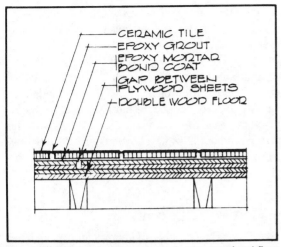

Fig. 2-10. Epoxy mortar and grout over wood subfloor (courtesy Tile Council of America).

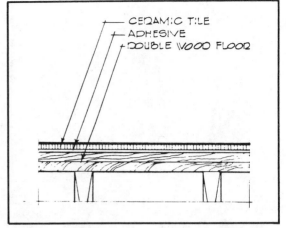

Fig. 2-12. Organic adhesive over wood subfloor (courtesy Tile Council of America).

Ceramic tile and similar floor coverings may be installed by the cement-plaster method or with adhesives. The cement-plaster method requires a concrete-cement setting bed of 1 1/4 inches minimum thickness (Fig. 2-3). Joists are beveled and cleats used to support waterproof plywood subfloor or forms cut between the joists. The cement base is reinforced with woven wire fabric or expanded metal lath.

The tile is normally soaked before it is installed.

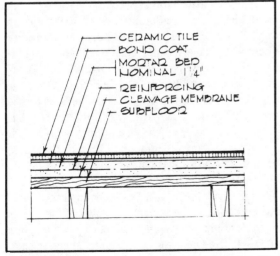

Fig. 2-11. Cement mortar over wood subfloor (courtesy Tile Council of America).

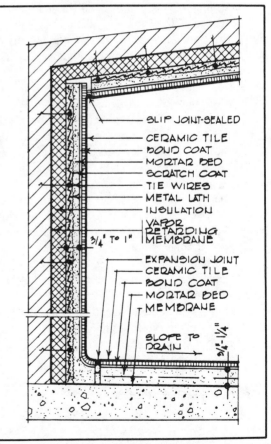

Fig. 2-13. Installing ceramic tile in a steam room (courtesy Tile Council of America).

49

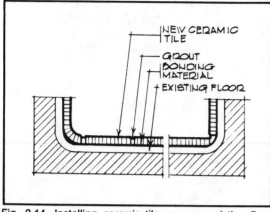

Fig. 2-14. Installing ceramic tile over an existing floor (courtesy Tile Council of America).

It is pressed firmly in place in the still plastic setting bed; mortar is compressed in the joints, and the joints tooled the same day tile is laid. Laying tile in this manner normally requires a workman skilled in this system. In Chapter 4 you will learn the method used by most do-it-yourselfers.

Adhesive used for ceramic floor tile should be the type recommended by the manufacturer. When installed over wood joists, a waterproof plywood that is 3/4-inch thick with perimeter and intermediate nailing provides a good base. Before you install tile, a waterproof sealer or a thin coat of tile adhesive must be applied to the plywood.

Tile is best set over a full covering of adhesive using the *floating method* with a slight twisting movement for full embedment. *Buttering,* or using small pats of adhesive on each tile, is not acceptable. Tile should not be grouted or filled between until volatiles from adhesive have evaporated. After grouting, joints should be fully tooled.

Again, this general information on installation is offered as an overview to guide you in planning your tile floor. Specific instructions will be offered in Chapters 3 and 4.

ESTIMATING TILE NEEDS

A simple square or rectangular room requires only minimal math to estimate the amount of floor tile needed. The length of the room is multiplied by the width (i.e., 9 × 12 feet) in order to find out the total floor area (108 square feet). It's then a matter of knowing the size and spacing of the selected tiles.

Many rooms, however, are not as simple to estimate. Figures 2-15 through 2-19 and Table 2-1 give an illustration of how various rooms can be easily measured for square footage. Because many installations of tile floors will also coincide with the installation of tile walls, showers, and countertops, Figs. 2-20 through 2-30 illustrate the methods for estimating such areas.

SELECTING TILE TOOLS

There are a number of general and specialized tools available for the installation of resilient and hard tile floors. Many are so specialized that they are difficult to find except in the tool boxes of professional tile installers. Fortunately, new tile designs and manufacturing methods have made such tools nearly obsolete and rarely vital to the do-it-yourselfer. Most of the tools you will need are either in your shop now or readily available.

Figures 2-31 through 2-34 illustrate popular tile installation tool kits available for most common floor tiles. They include both tools and related materials needed for a professional-looking tile floor.

You can also purchase the tools you need individuality. Figure 2-35 illustrates a tool common to a variety of do-it-yourself jobs, and therefore likely to be in many tool boxes: the chalk line. Perhaps the most convenient type of chalk line is the kind with a metal box or case. The box keeps the line clean when not in use and also holds an ample supply of chalk which adheres to the line as it is pulled from the box. After use, it may be returned to the box by means of a small crank or winding handle. The box or case may also serve as a plumb bob.

The chalk line is used to mark finish and working lines where tile is being installed. The line is stretched tightly between two predetermined points and then lifted near the center and allowed to snap back against the surface, thus depositing a thin line of chalk dust. The dust can readily be removed

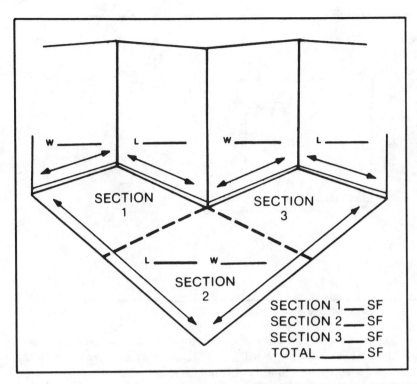

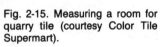

Fig. 2-15. Measuring a room for quarry tile (courtesy Color Tile Supermart).

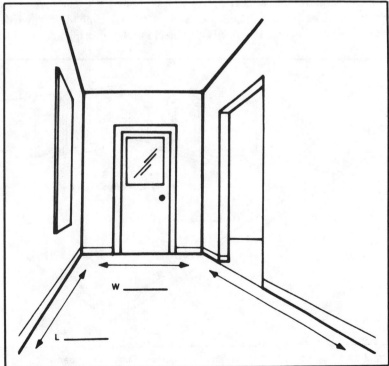

Fig. 2-16. Measuring a hallway for quarry tile (courtesy Color Tile Supermart).

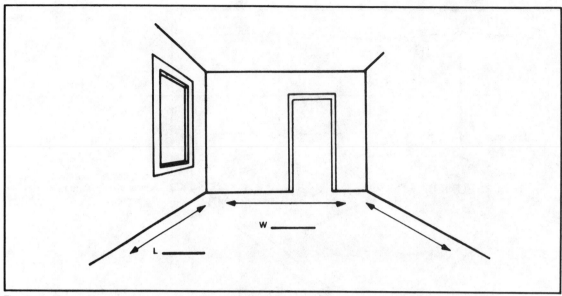

Fig. 2-17. Measuring a square room (courtesy Color Tile Supermart).

from most surfaces when no longer needed.

In order to do efficient work, the do-it-yourself tile setter should have at least one level (Fig. 2-36). The 24-inch level is the most convenient and will work for most jobs. In some cases, though, a smaller level of about 9 inches is a valuable tool.

When working on large areas, a 48-inch mason's level will give more accuracy and save considerable time in obtaining a true line.

The level must be checked for accuracy from time to time, particularly if it is an adjustable one. Jarring and pounding on the level will impair its ac-

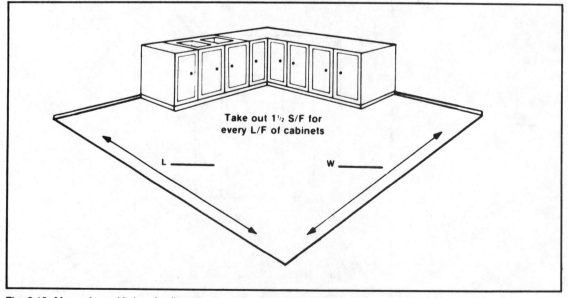

Fig. 2-18. Measuring a kitchen for floor tile (courtesy Color Tile Supermart).

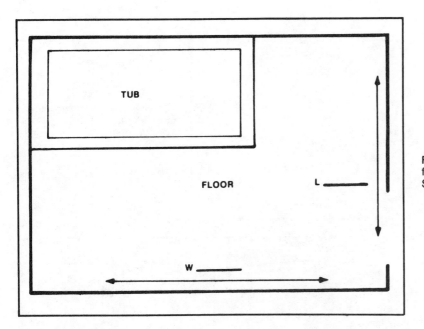

FLOOR

TUB

L _____

W _____

Fig. 2-19. Measuring a bathroom for floor tile (courtesy Color Tile Supermart).

curacy, making it necessary to readjust. The simplest way to check a level is to reverse it. If the reading is the same either way, there is no need for adjustment. The level should never be hit with another tool, nor should it ever be used as a screed for leveling off mortar.

The combination square (Fig. 2-37) is a small square with an adjustable head and usually 1- × -12-inch blade grooved to fit the keeper in the head of the square. A thumbscrew adjustment permits you to lock the head at any point along the blade. The long part of the head is at right angles to the blade. Opposite this is a beveled side which

forms a 45-degree angle with the blade. High-grade squares have a level glass placed just above the margin of the long side of the head. At the end of the head, opposite the blade, is often a small scriber. This piece is fitted with a rounded knob to facilitate withdrawing it from the head. The scriber is useful in marking metal and other hard surfaces, such as tile.

The claw hammer (Fig. 2-38) is another common tool that is used by the tile installer. It is used for nailing on paper and metal lath, installing subflooring, and "chipping." A chipping hammer can also be used to chip away excess materials from

Table 2-1. Ceramic Tile Estimating Table (courtesy Color Tile Supermart).

Example _____

FLOOR: W _____ × _____ L = _____ S/F
FLOOR: W _____ × _____ L = _____ S/F
FLOOR: W _____ × _____ L = _____ S/F
FLOOR: W _____ × _____ L = _____ S/F
FLOOR: W _____ × _____ L = _____ S/F
NOTE: Subtract 12 S/F for tub _____ S/F
　　　　　　　TOTAL: _____

NOTE:
4 × 8 = 11 S/F Per Carton: 4.5 Pcs. Per S/F
6 × 6 = 11 S/F Per Carton: 4 Pcs. Per S/F
8 × 8 = 11 S/F Per Carton: 2.25 Pcs. Per S/F
10 × 10 = 11 S/F Per Carton: 1.44 Pcs. Per S/F
12 × 12 = 11 S/F Per Carton: 1 Pc. Per S/F
NOTE: If figuring with inches Total inches ÷ by 144
　　　　　= S/F "Tile"

Total inches ÷ by 12
　= L/F "Trim"

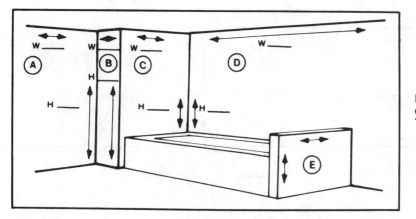

Fig. 2-20. Measuring bathroom for ceramic wall tile (courtesy Color Tile Supermart).

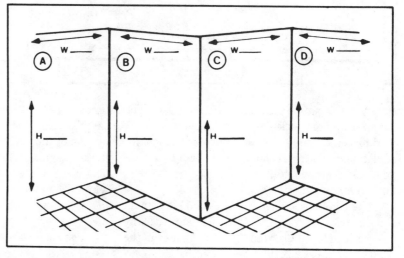

Fig. 2-21. Measuring short walls for ceramic tile (courtesy Color Tile Supermart).

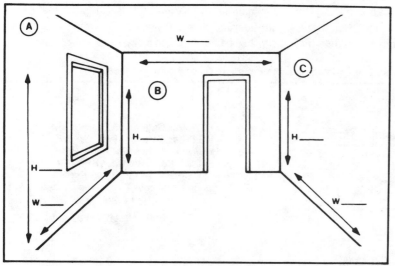

Fig. 2-22. Measuring typical room for ceramic wall tile (courtesy Color Tile Supermart).

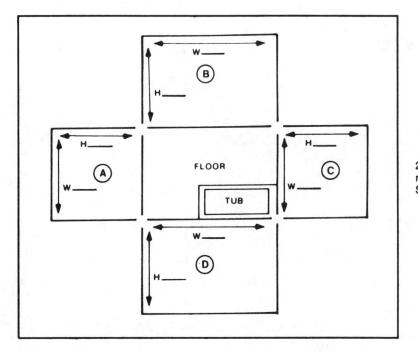

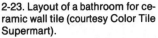

2-23. Layout of a bathroom for ceramic wall tile (courtesy Color Tile Supermart).

the back of the tile and along the edges.

The pry bar (Fig. 2-39) is primarily used to pry tiles together or to remove old flooring materials. Figure 2-40 illustrates three tile cutting tools. Tile nippers (Fig. 2-41) look much like the carpenter's nail pullers. You can even use a nail puller if you don't have tile nippers. The tile nipper is used to take small bites out of ceramic and other hard tiles. Remember to only take small bites because big bites with tile nippers may cause the tile to crack and break. It is usually best to score the tile either with a glass cutter or a tile cutting board before attempting the cut.

The tile cutter (Fig. 2-42) is one of the most ef-

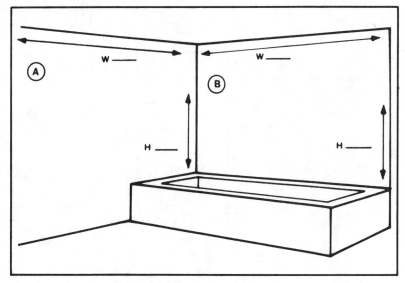

Fig. 2-24. Measuring walls for ceramic tile around the bathroom tub (courtesy Color Tile Supermart).

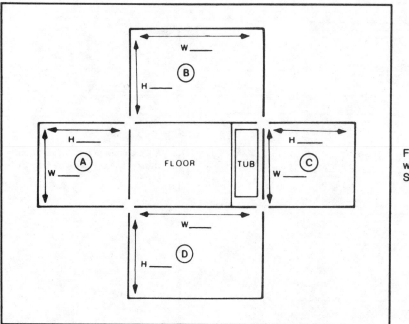

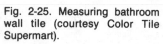

Fig. 2-25. Measuring bathroom wall tile (courtesy Color Tile Supermart).

Fig. 2-26. Measuring a show stall for ceramic wall tile (courtesy Color Tile Supermart).

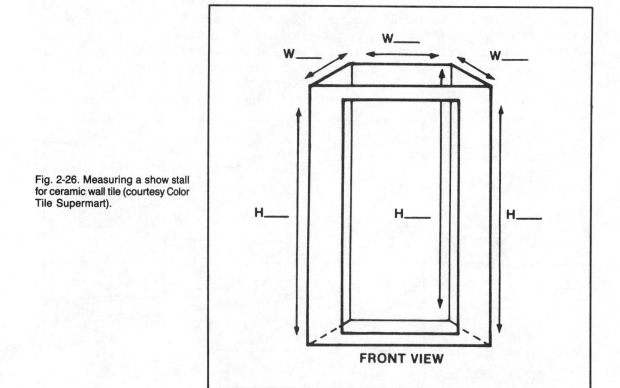

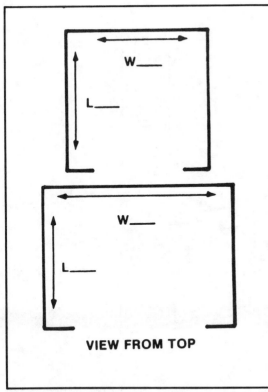

Fig. 2-27. Layout for a shower stall (courtesy Color Tile Supermart).

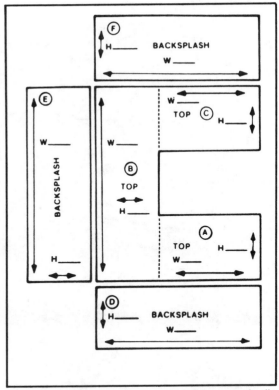

Fig. 2-28. Layout of kitchen countertop for ceramic tile (courtesy Color Tile Supermart).

ficient and economical tools for cutting hard tiles. One type consists of an aluminum base with a steel bar above, along with a slotted handle fitted with a glass cutter cluster arranged to slide back and forth as the cut is made. The clusters usually consist of three or six tiny wheels which may be brought to use as one becomes dull. The board is fitted with a rib in the center that is in line with the cutters. The breaking bar exerts pressure over this rib to break the scored tile. Rubber pads at each side of the center rib provide cushions to reduce the shock and prevent breaking in any direction except that desired. The slotted part of the handle and the steel guide should be slightly oiled to keep the action free. The board is equipped with an angle gauge for 45- and 90-degree angles. Other angles may be obtained by adjusting the gauge to the cut desired.

An electric tile saw is also available, but is usually not used by the do-it-yourselfer. Tile cutters may also be rented or borrowed from tile retailers.

Figure 2-43 illustrates a tile snapper. It will break the typical ceramic tile along the score line when depressed.

Figure 2-44 shows a typical grout trowel used to wipe excess grout from tile surfaces. There are many other types of trowels for spreading the adhesives and grouts used in tile installation.

Those are the most common tools used to install tile flooring. Most of them are specifically for the installation of hard tiles because resilient tile flooring is much simpler to install and usually requires little more than a chalk line, some snips, and possibly an adhesive spreader. In many cases, the tiles are self-adhesive-backed, making the job very easy.

Probably the most difficult task for the do-it-

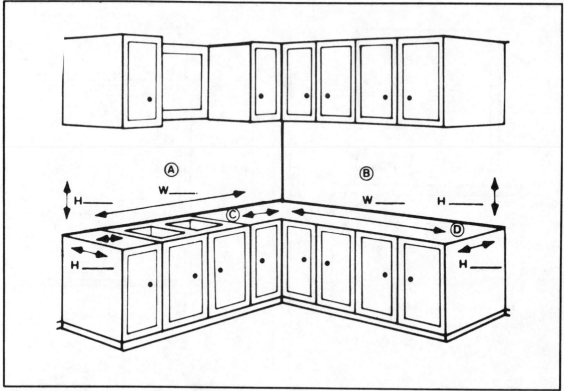

Fig. 2-29. Planning countertop tile installation (courtesy Color Tile Supermart).

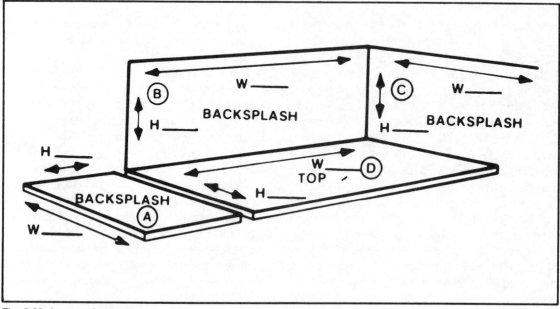

Fig. 2-30. Layout of straight run countertop (courtesy Color Tile Supermart).

Fig. 2-31. Typical floor tile installation kit.

yourself tile floor installer is cutting hard tiles. Let's consider the best ways to make professional cuts.

CUTTING TILE

If there is no tile saw or cutting board available, tile may be cut with a glass cutter. The glass cutter gives you two pieces, whereas if the tile is cut with a tile nipper, only one piece is obtained.

The tools you'll need include a glass cutter, a steel rule, and a chisel. First, place a straightedge along the line of cut. Next, hold the glass cutter upright and bring it toward you along the edge of the straightedge. Be sure that the straightedge doesn't slip. Now make only one cut along the desired line. Repeating will tend to chip the glaze too much. After you've scored the tile, break it over a chisel.

When it's necessary to cut a small amount off the edges of tile in order to make them fit a given

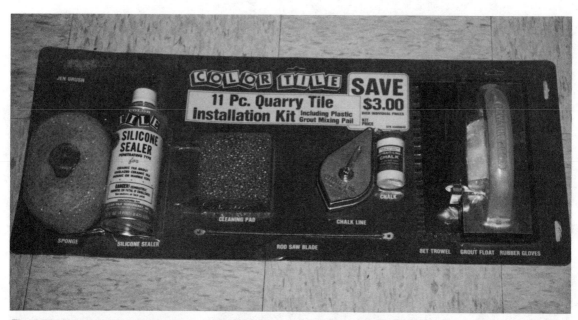

Fig. 2-32. Quarry tile installation kit.

area, the tile nippers are the most convenient. The same job can be done with the tile saw if you have one.

You'll need tile nippers, a pencil, and a folding rule. First, mark the line along which the tile is to be cut. Next, hold the tile with your left hand and the nippers in your right hand. Then begin the cut with the jaws of the nippers gripping the tile at half their width, rather than taking a full bite. Now hold the lower jaw of the nippers slightly forward. Exert a little pressure downward on the handles as you squeeze them together. This will tend to break the tile chips on a bevel and away from the line of the cut.

Cut the tile carefully to avoid excessive grinding. Taking bites that are too large will cause the tile to break in the wrong direction. It is better to take a small bite each time and work up to the desired line. This will help when you are making a notched cut, as you must when installing hard tile around pipes or other plumbing.

The tile cutter (Fig. 2-42) is a mechanical device provided with guides and scoring wheels. It reduces the time involved in cutting hard tile. To cut with the tile cutter, first place the tile at the back

edge of the cutter and against the rear guide. Next move the adjustable gauge to the side of the tile and lock it when the mark for the cut is directly below the cutting wheel. Then grasp the handle firmly with your right hand and, beginning at the edge farthest from you, bring the cutter toward you. The result will be a neat score that needs only to be broken.

The handle of the tile cutter has an extension at the bottom that runs at right angles to the handle itself. This is the breaking bar. The narrow rib that runs parallel with and directly beneath the guide bar serves the same purpose in breaking as does a chisel. Press down on the handle until the breaking bar is touching the tile and then, with a quick pressure, continue the movement downward. The tile will break neatly along the desired line if it is scored deeply enough and aligned properly with the breaking rip. Make both parallel and diagonal cuts in this manner because guides are provided for various types of cutting.

FLOOR TILE ADHESIVES

There are numerous adhesives available for the installation of resilient and hard tile flooring (Figs.

60

2-45 and 2-46 and Table 2-2). Basically, *mortar* is a combination of sand, cement, either fireclay or lime, and water. It's primarily used as a thick adhesive into which hard tiles are set. Tile *adhesive* is a thinner substance spread on the subfloor and onto which the resilient or hard tile is laid. Some types of resilient tile have *self-adhesive* on the underside which can be activated by simply pealing off

a cover sheet. *Grout* is a thin, coarse mortar used for filling the space between hard tiles.

While the selection of mortar, adhesive, and grout will be dictated by the type of tile flooring you select as well as manufacturers' and retailers' suggestions, you should know what's available and how they work. Let's take mortar, adhesive, and grout separately.

Fig. 2-33. Ceramic tile installation kit.

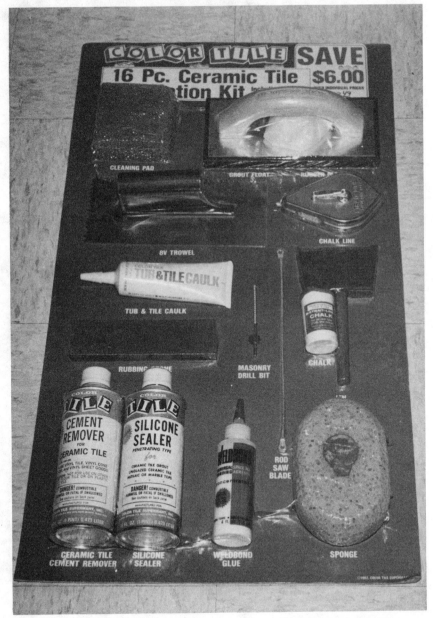

Fig. 2-34. Mosaic tile installation kit.

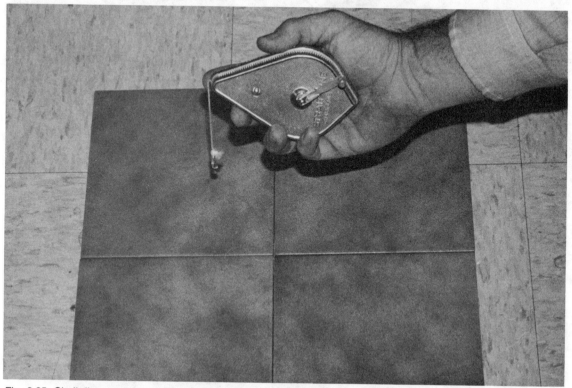

Fig. 2-35. Chalk line used for marking floors prior to tile installation.

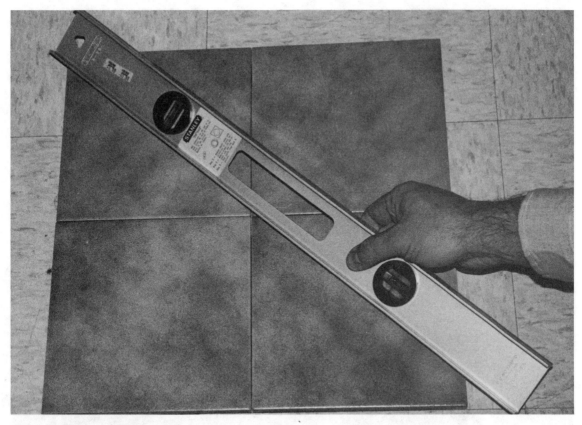

Fig. 2-36. Carpenter's level.

SELECTING TILE MORTAR

There are six common types of mortar used in the installation of hard tiles, each having its own unique properties and applications:

Portland Cement Mortar. A mixture of portland cement and sand on floors, and of portland cement, sand, and lime for walls. Portland cement mortar is suitable for most surfaces and ordinary types of installation. The thick bed, 3/4 to 1 inch on walls and 3/4 to 1 1/4 inches on floors, facilitates accurate slopes or planes in the finished tile work. Proportions are given on the packages.

Dry-Set Mortar. A mixture of portland cement with sand and additives imparting water retentivity that is used as a bond coat for setting tile. Dry-set mortar is suitable for use over a variety of surfaces. It is used in one layer, as thin as 3/32 inch, after tiles are beat in, has excellent wa-

ter and impact resistance, can be cleaned with water, is nonflammable, is good for exterior work, and doesn't required soaking of tile.

Latex-Portland Cement Mortar. A mixture of portland cement, sand, and special latex additive that is used as a bond coat for setting tile. The uses for latex-portland cement mortar are similar to those of dry-set mortar. It is less rigid than portland cement mortar. Latex-portland cement mortar is used to install ceramic tile in an area that may not thoroughly dry out in use, such as swimming pools and gang showers. It is recommended that the completed installation be allowed to thoroughly dry out before it is exposed to water. This drying period can fluctuate from 14 to over 60 days depending upon the geographical location, the climate conditions, and whether the installation is interior or exterior.

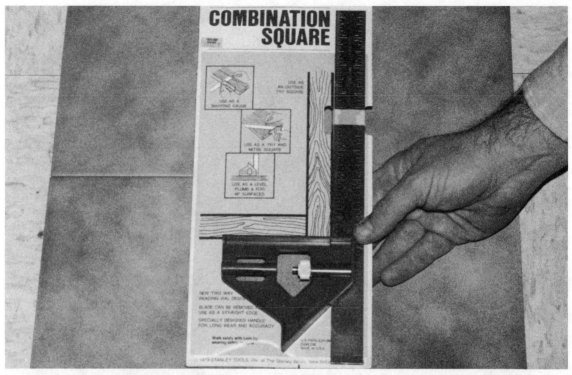

Fig. 2-37. Combination square.

Fig. 2-38. Claw hammer.

64

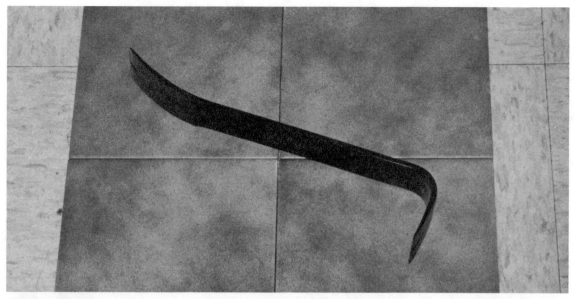

Fig. 2-39. Pry bar.

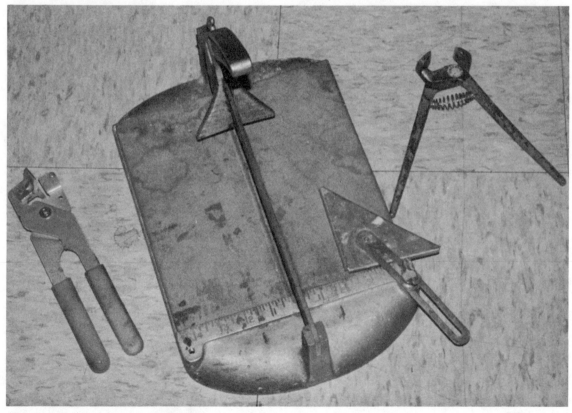

Fig. 2-40. Three common tile cutting tools.

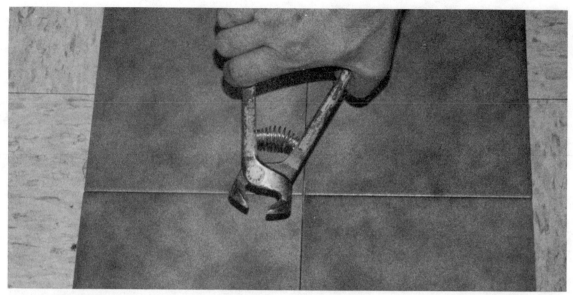

Fig. 2-41. Tile nippers.

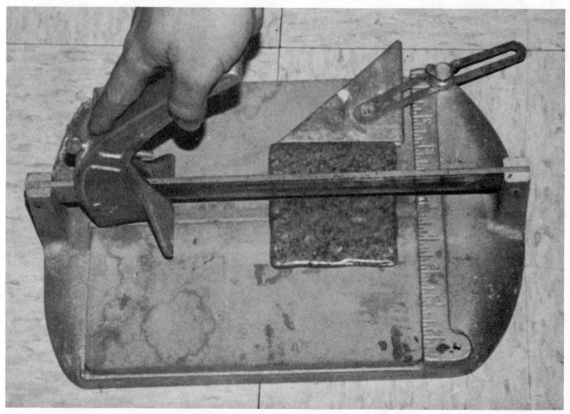

Fig. 2-42. Tile cutter ready to score the tile.

66

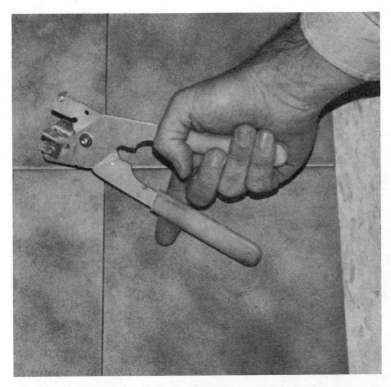

Fig. 2-43. Tile snappers.

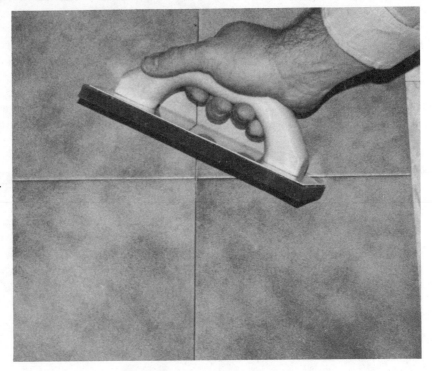

Fig. 2-44. Tile grout trowel.

Fig. 2-45. Floor and wall primer.

Epoxy Mortar. A mortar system employing epoxy resin and epoxy hardener portions. Epoxy mortar is suitable for use where chemical resistance of floors, high bond strength, and high impact resistance are important considerations. Acceptable subfloors when properly prepared include concrete, wood and plywood, steel plate, and ceramic tile. Application is made in one thin layer.

Modified Epoxy Emulsion Mortars. A mortar/grout system employing emulsified epoxy resins and hardeners with portland cement and silica sand. Modified epoxy emulsion mortars are formulated for thin-set installations of ceramic tile on floors and walls, interior and exterior. Their features include high bond strength, ease of application, little or no shrinkage, and economical epoxy application. They are not designed for chemical resistance, but are better than portland cement mor-

tars or organic adhesives. Recommended uses include residential and light-duty floors over substrates such as plywood and concrete. This material is recommended by most manufacturers as a bond coat or setting material. Some also recommend it for grouting. Properties vary with the manufacturer.

Furan Mortar. A mortar system consisting of furan resin and furan hardener portions. Furan mortar is suitable for use where chemical resistance of floors is an important consideration. Acceptable subfloors when properly prepared include concrete, wood and plywood, steel plate, and ceramic tile. Properties vary with the manufacturer.

SELECTING TILE ADHESIVE

There are basically two broad types of adhesive used in the installation of tile: epoxy and organic.

Epoxy Adhesive. An adhesive system employing epoxy resin and epoxy hardener portions. Epoxy adhesive is formulated for thin-setting of tile on floors, walls, and counters with epoxy as the major binder. It is designed primarily for high bond strength and ease of application and not for optimum chemical resistance. Its chemical and solvent resistance, however, tends to be better than that of organic adhesives.

Organic Adhesive. A prepared organic material, ready to use with no further addition of liquid or powder, which cures or sets by evaporation. Organic adhesive is suitable for installing tile on floors, walls, and counters where surfaces are appropriate and properly prepared. Adhesives are applied in one thin layer with a trowel, first using the flat edge for continuous coverage and then the notched edge for uniform thickness. Where leveling or truing is required, an underlayment is used.

Adhesives eliminate the soaking of tile. They are not suitable for swimming pools or exteriors, but are often used for residential floors. They supply some flexibility to the tile facing. Bond strength varies greatly among the numerous brands available.

SELECTING TILE GROUT

Grouting materials for ceramic tile are available

Fig. 2-46. Adhesive caulks for tile installation.

in many forms to meet the requirements of the different kinds of tile and types of exposures. Portland cement is the base for most grouts and is modified to provide specific qualities such as whiteness, mildew resistance, uniformity, hardness, flexibility, and water retentivity. Noncement based grouts, such as epoxies, furans, and silicon rubber, offer properties not possible with cement grouts. Special skills on the part of the setter are often required, however.

Commercial Portland Cement Grout. A mixture of portland cement and other ingredients to produce a water-resistant dense, uniformly colored material. The floor type of grout, usually gray, is designed for use with ceramic mosaics, quarry, and paver tiles. The wall type, usually white, is designed for conventional mortar installations with a very fine variety of aggregate. Damp curing is required for both floor and wall types.

Sand-Portland Cement Grout. An on-the-job mixture of 1 part portland cement to 1 part fine graded sand is used for joints up to 1/8 inch wide; 1 to 2 for joints up to 1/2 inch wide; and 1 to 3 for for joints over 1/2 inch wide. Up to 1/5 part lime may be added. Sand-portland cement grout is used with ceramic mosaic tile, quarry, and paver tile on floors and walls. Damp curing is necessary.

Dry-Set Grout. A mixture of portland cement

Table 2-2. Grout Guide (Courtesy Tile Council of America).

Printed through the courtesy of the Materials & Methods Standards Association

A rubber faced trowel should be used when grouting glazed tile with sanded grout.

	Commercial Portland Cement — Wall Use	Commercial Portland Cement — Floor Use	Sand-Portland Cement — Wall-Floor Use	Dry-Set — Wall-Floor Use	Latex Portland Cement (3)	Mastic (3)	Epoxy (1)(6)	Furan (1)(6)	Silicone or Urethane (2)	Modified Epoxy Emulsion (3)(6)
TILE TYPE										
GLAZED WALL TILE (More than 7% absorption)	●					●			●	●
CERAMIC MOSAICS	●	●	●	●	●	●	●	●	●	●
QUARRY, PAVER & PACKING HOUSE TILE	●	●	●	●	●		●	●		●
AREAS OF USE										
Dry and intermittently wet areas	●	●	●	●	●	●	●	●	●	●
Areas subject to prolonged wetting	●	●	●	●	●		●	●	●	●
Exteriors	●	●	●	●	●(4)		●(4)	●(4)		●(4)
PERFORMANCE										
Stain Resistance (5)	D	C	E	D	B	A	A	A	A	B
Crack Resistance (5)	D	D	E	D	C	C	B	C	A Flexible	C
Colorability (5)	B	B	C	B	B	A	B	Black Only	Restricted	B

(1) Mainly used for chemical resistant properties.
(2) Special tools needed for proper application. Silicone, urethane and modified polyvinylchloride used in pregrouted ceramic tile sheets. Silicone grout should not be used on kitchen countertops or other food preparation surfaces unless it meets the requirements of FDA Regulation No. 21, CFE 177.2600.
(3) Special cleaning procedures and materials recommended.
(4) Follow manufacturer's directions.
(5) Five performance ratings — Best to Minimal (A B C D E).
(6) Epoxies are recommended for prolonged temperatures up to 140F, high temperature resistant epoxies and furans up to 350F.

and additives providing water retentivity, dry-set grout has the same characteristics as dry-set mortar (covered earlier). It is suitable for grouting all floors and walls subject to ordinary use. This grout eliminates the soaking of tile, although dampening is sometimes required under very dry conditions. Damp curing may develop greater strength in portland cement grouts.

Latex-Portland Cement Grout. A mixture of any one of the three preceding grouts with special latex additive. Latex-portland cement grout is suitable for all installations subject to ordinary use and for most commercial installations of hard tile floors. It is less absorptive than regular cement grout.

Mastic Grout. A one-part grouting composition that is used directly from the container. Mastic grout hardens by coalescence and doesn't require damp curing as do portland cement based grouts. It is more flexible and stain-resistant than regular cement grout.

Furan Resin Grout. A grout system consisting of furan resin and hardener portions, primarily for quarry tile, packing house tile, and paver tile. Furan grout is used in industrial and commercial areas requiring chemical resistance. Use of this grout involves extra costs, including waxing tile surface, and special installation skills when compared to portland cement grouts.

Epoxy Grout. A grouting system employing epoxy resin and hardener portions, often containing coarse silica filler, especially formulated for industrial and commercial installations. This grout provides chemical resistance, high bond strength, and impact resistance. High-temperature/chemical-resistant formulas are also available. They impart structural qualities to the tile when used both as a mortar and grout, especially over wood subfloors. They are more expensive to install than portland cement grouts.

Silicon Rubber Grout. An engineered elastomeric grout system for interior use employing a single component of nonslumping silicon rubber. When cured it is resistant to staining, moisture, mildew, cracking, crazing, and shrinking. This grout adheres tenaciously to ceramic tile without primers; cures rapidly; withstands exposure to hot cooking oils, free steam, and oxygen, and withstands prolonged exposure to subfreezing temperatures and hot humid conditions. Silicon rubber grout is more costly but can be very practical for many floor and wall installations.

RESILIENT TILE ADHESIVES

Adhesives for resilient tile vary greatly depending upon the composition of the tile itself and the subfloor on which it is to be applied. In many cases, such as self-stick resilient tiles, the selection of the correct adhesive is made for you. In other cases, the adhesive is suggested by the manufacturer or the retailer. It's best to take this advice, which was developed through chemical testing and laboratory application. If possible, stay with the brand suggested by the manufacturer because each brand will have a slightly different composition and may react differently when applied.

Installing Resilient Tile Floors

Resilient tile floors are the most popular with the do-it-yourselfer because they are easy to install. They are also less expensive than hard tile or wood floors—the typical cost is $75 to $125 per room.

Resilient tile floors come in two types defined by the method of installation or adhesion: self-adhering and dry-back. *Self-adhering tile* flooring is simply tiles with a backing that can be pulled away to expose an adhesive. *Dry-back tile* must have the adhesive spread on the floor or the back of the tile in order to be installed. Otherwise, installation is very similar.

REMOVING THE EXISTING FLOOR

The first step in the installation of a resilient tile floor is the removal of any existing flooring. This step isn't required for new construction or an add-on room. Carpeting can be easily pulled up and tack strips removed, but in many cases, an earlier resilient tile or sheet flooring must be removed.

First, a word of warning: don't sand existing resilient flooring, backing, or lining felt. These pro-

ducts may contain asbestos fibers that are not readily identifiable. Inhalation of asbestos dust may damage lungs, especially if you also smoke.

To remove existing sheet flooring, the wear layer should first be cut into narrow strips. Be careful not to score the underlayment if it is a wood subfloor. The narrow strips should then be peeled off from the backing by pulling or rolling around a core, that will control the stripping angle and create a uniform tension. Some resilient flooring wear layers may not be readily strippable and could require scraping.

After the wear layer has been removed, examine the remaining felt to determine whether or not it will serve as a suitable base for the new floor covering. Areas where the felt is not adhered should be cut open and rebound. Areas where the backing pulls free should be leveled using a latex underlayment.

If the remaining felt is not suitable, it should be removed by wet scraping. Moisten the felt with a water solution of dishwashing detergent. The solution should be applied to the felt backing and allowed to penetrate for several minutes before you scrape. Only enough solution should be used to keep the top surface of the backing damp. Therefore, more than one application may be necessary, depending upon the time required for removal.

Proper care must be exercised in the cleanup and disposal of all waste material during the resilient flooring removal process. This material should be placed in heavy-duty plastic trash bags or similar containers to minimize dust generation. Exposed floor areas should be cleaned with a wet-dry vacuum cleaner.

Remember not to soak the felt because excessive moisture can cause permanent damage to wood underlayments. A floor that has been wet-scraped must be allowed to dry before you install the resilient flooring.

INSTALLING SELF-ADHERING TILE

The installation of self-adhering, or self-stick, resilient floor tile is very simple (Fig. 3-1). For best color match when using tiles from two or more packages, check to be sure all pattern and lot numbers are the same.

For proper installation, floors must be smooth and completely free of wax, grease, and dirt. Dusty concrete subfloors should be vacuumed. Firmly bonded paint and smooth-surface resilient floors are acceptable bases for self-adhering floor tiles. Embossed no-wax urethane floors or cushioned floors are not acceptable and should be removed. Particleboard, frequently called *chipboard*, is sometimes used as a type of underlayment. Results of the bonding may not be satisfactory, however; so many manufacturers recommend that you do not lay self-adhering tile flooring over particleboard. In most cases, you can install such flooring over suspended, on-grade, and below-grade floors and over terrazzo floors.

Never install flooring tiles over a subfloor that is wet or damp. The surface of the subfloor must be dry to ensure a good adhesive bond. Install in an area having a minimum temperature of 65 degrees Fahrenheit for at least 48 hours before and during installation and for 48 hours after installation. Thereafter, a minimum temperature of 55 degrees should be maintained to help establish a firm bond to the subfloor.

First, pry up molding at the base of walls so that tiles can be placed underneath during installation. Next, find the center for each of the end walls. Connect these points by striking a chalk line down the middle of the floor. This is the *center chalk line* (Fig. 3-2).

Locate the center of this line. Now, using a tile, draw a perpendicular line. On this perpendicular, strike a chalk line connecting the two sidewalls. The floor is now divided into quarters (Fig. 3-3). Next, place a row of tiles along the perpendicular chalk line from the center of the room to the sidewall, but don't remove the release paper (Fig. 3-4).

Measure the distance between the sidewall and the last full tile. If the space is less than half the width of a tile, strike a new chalk line beside the old center chalk line half the width of a tile either toward or away from the wall. This will give even borders on both sides of the room. Repeat the procedure on the end wall. The point where the two chalk lines cross is the starting point for installing tiles (Fig. 3-5).

Now remove the release paper from each tile as you install it (Fig. 3-6). Start placing tiles at the center point. Make sure that the edges are even with the chalk line and each tile is butted against adjoining pieces (Fig. 3-7). Do not slide tiles into place. Press the tiles firmly into place as you install them. For best appearance, install each embossed tile with the arrows on the back all pointing in the same direction (Fig. 3-8). Cover the first quarter of the room with the exception of the border area where the tiles must be cut to fit.

To cut and fit tiles next to the walls, place a loose tile (Fig. 3-9A) exactly on top of the last full tile in any row. On top of this, place a third tile (Fig. 3-9B) and slide it until it butts against the wall. Using the edge of the top as a guide, mark the tile under it with a pencil. Then use a straight-blade utility knife or a sturdy pair of household shears (Fig. 3-10) to cut along this line. To fit pieces of

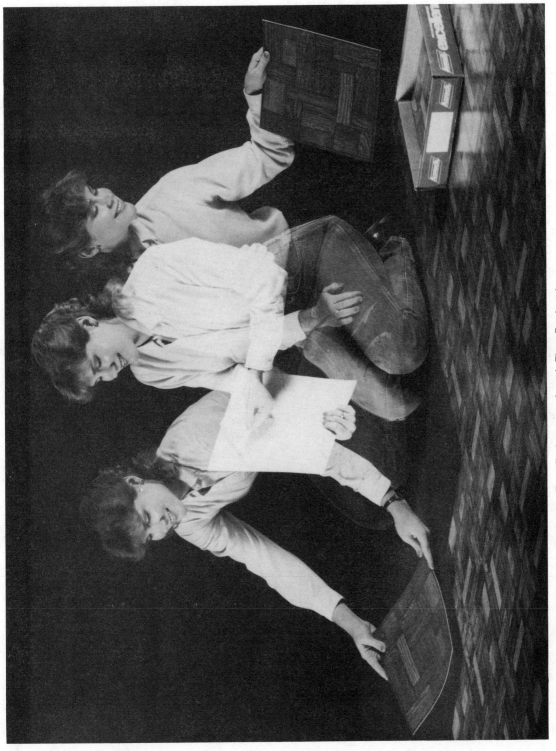

Fig. 3-1. Typical installation of vinyl self-adhering floor tile (courtesy Azrock Floor Products).

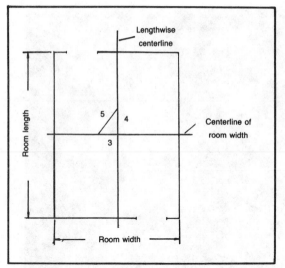

Fig. 3-2. Finding the center chalk line.

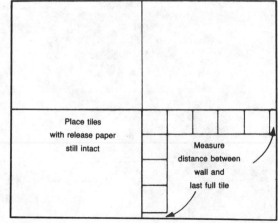

Fig. 3-4. Laying self-adhering floor tiles (courtesy Armstrong World Industries).

tile around pipes or other irregularities, make a pattern of the proper shape from paper, trace it on the tile, and cut.

Finally, repeat these steps for the remaining three quarters of the room. In just a few hours the job is completed, and your room has a new resilient tile floor (Fig. 3-11).

INSTALLING DRY-BACK FLOOR TILE

The installation procedures for a dry-back resilient tile floor is much the same as that for a self-

adhering tile floor. Make sure that your base floor or subfloor is ready for the installation, that the old flooring (if any) is removed or prepared, and that the area is clean. These steps will ensure good adhesion of the new flooring tiles.

To locate the center of the room, find the center of each wall, then pull a chalked string taut to the opposite wall across the center of the room. Snap a straight line on the subfloor (Fig. 3-12) to allow the room to be *squared off* so that the tile is laid parallel to the walls.

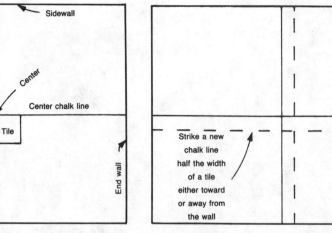

Fig. 3-3. Divide the floor into quarters (courtesy Armstrong World Industries).

Fig. 3-5. Adjusted chalk line for beginning the installation (courtesy Armstrong World Industries).

Fig. 3-6. Peel off the protective paper for installation (courtesy Armstrong World Industries).

Fig. 3-7. Maneuver the tile into position (courtesy Armstrong World Industries).

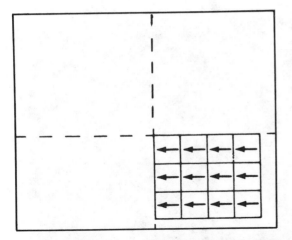

Fig. 3-8. Install tile with arrows on the back pointing in the same direction (courtesy Armstrong World Industries).

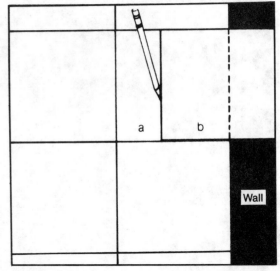

Fig. 3-9. Fitting a tile next to the wall (courtesy Armstrong World Industries).

To plan the floor (Fig. 3-13), lay a row of loose tiles along the chalk line from the center point to one sidewall and one end wall. Measure the distance between the wall and the last full tile. If this space is less than a half a tile wide, snap a new chalk line and move half a width of tile closer to the opposite wall. Check the right angles. Now, do the same with the other row. This will improve the appearance of the floor and eliminate the need to fit small pieces of tile next to the walls.

Check to make sure that you have the correct adhesive for your tile. Before spreading the adhesive, read the instruction label on the can. Spread the adhesive over one quarter of the area, bonded on two sides by the center chalk lines. Adhesive should be brushed, troweled, or rolled on thinly so that when the tile is laid, the adhesive will not push up between the tiles or cause them to slip underfoot (Fig. 3-14).

Allow the adhesive to set the recommended time and, starting at the center point, lay the tile in the adhesive (Fig. 3-15). One quarter section of the room is laid at a time, starting at the center point and moving toward one wall (Figs. 3-16 and 3-17). Each tile should be set down firmly and tightly to the adjoining tile so that there are no "joints" between the tiles. Don't slide the tiles into place or the adhesive may come up between the tiles.

To cut and fit the dry-back tile next to the wall, place a loose tile (Fig. 3-18A) squarely on top of the last full tile closest to the wall. On top of this, place a third tile (Fig. 3-18B) and slide it until it butts against the wall. Using the edge of the top tile as a guide, mark the tile under it with a pencil. With a pair of household shears, cut tile A along the pencil line.

To fit around pipes and other obstructions, make a paper pattern to fit the space exactly. Trace the outline onto the tile and cut with the shears. Insert tile into the border space with the rough edge against the wall (Fig. 3-19).

INSTALLING SHEET FLOORING

Although this book is written primarily for the do-it-yourselfer who is installing resilient and hard tile flooring, you may want to compare methods with or even install resilient sheet flooring. This section explains the procedure.

First, prepare the floor. Nail all loose boards, replace defective boards, fill cracks with wood filler, and remove all dirt, grease, wax, varnish, and paint.

In some cases, felt should first be laid to in-

Fig. 3-10. Using household shears to cut the tile (courtesy Armstrong World Industries).

Fig. 3-11. The completed self-adhering resilient tile floor (courtesy Armstrong World Industries).

Fig. 3-12. Snap a straight line on the subfloor (courtesy Azrock Floor Products).

Fig. 3-13. Lay loose tiles to plan the floor (courtesy Azrock Floor Products).

Fig. 3-14. Spreading adhesive for dry-back resilient floor tile (courtesy Azrock Floor Products).

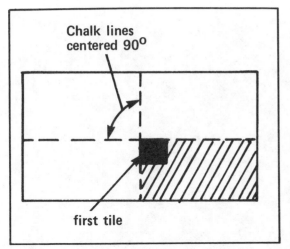

Chalk lines centered 90°

first tile

Fig. 3-15. Spread the adhesive for one section, then lay the first tile.

crease the life of the flooring covering. Unroll the first strips across the floor boards, not along the boards. Cut strips to fit around pipes and other projections and baseboards at each end. Butt the second strip to the first. Never overlap. When strips have been fitted to the whole room, roll them all back halfway. Spread adhesive on the floor with a spreader to the thickness recommended by the manufacturer. Then roll the felt strips back over the paste and repeat the adhesive application for the other half of the room. After all felt is pasted, roll it with a rolling pin, putting your body weight

heavily on it. Leave the felt to set for 2 or 3 hours before you lay sheet flooring. Note that concrete floors should not have felt.

Standard sheet flooring many times comes in rolls that are 72 inches wide. The piece to be fitted runs from end to end of the room and butts side baseboards.

First, unroll the sheet flooring across floor boards and parallel to felt, if any. Next, cut the piece at least 2 inches longer than the room. Then place the piece so it rides up 1 inch on each end baseboard. Now pull the piece out from the side baseboard so it lies flat.

Strap chalk to the inside of one leg of the carpenter's dividers with tape. Set dividers so the sharp point sets firmly at the joint between the baseboard and floor and the chalk point rests 1 inch inside the edge of the sheet. Start at one end of the sheet and draw a chalk line the whole length (Fig. 3-20). Now cut the sheet flooring along the line.

To fit sheet flooring around a pipe (Fig. 3-21), measure the distance from A in the illustration from the nearest end baseboard to the pipe and transfer the distance to the flooring (A′). Then measure distance B from the pipe to the side baseboard and transfer to the flooring (B′). Cut the pattern to the shape of the pipe entry at the floor and lay on the flooring in the correct place. Cut around the pattern neatly. Cut a slip from the edge of the sheet to the hole so the sheet flooring can be fitted around

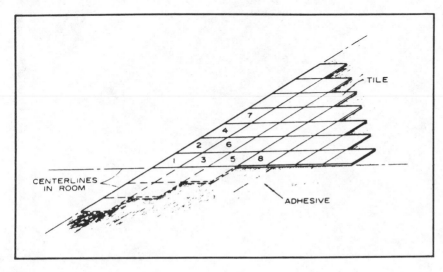

TILE

CENTERLINES IN ROOM

ADHESIVE

Fig. 3-16. Laying out the first tiles.

Fig. 3-17. Continuing the installation of tiles (courtesy Azrock Floor Products).

Armstrong Glazecraft luxury no-wax floor tile in southfork/white (courtesy Armstrong World Industries, Inc.).

Armstrong Roman Court solarian tile (courtesy Armstrong World Industries, Inc.).

Armstrong Glazecraft luxury no-wax floor tile on both the floor and wall in Hilltop/clover (courtesy Armstrong World Industries, Inc.).

Armstrong Glazecraft luxury no-wax floor tile in Center Square/walnut and Center Square/cream (courtesy Armstrong World Industries, Inc.).

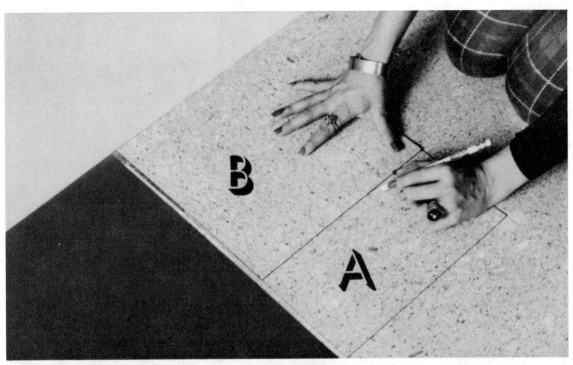

Fig. 3-18. Fitting tiles next to the wall (courtesy Azrock Floor Products).

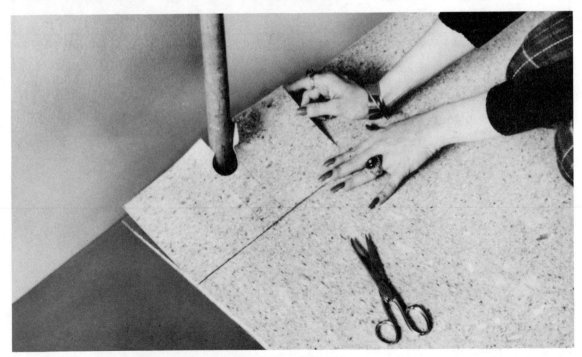

Fig. 3-19. Fitting tiles around a pipe (courtesy Azrock Floor Products).

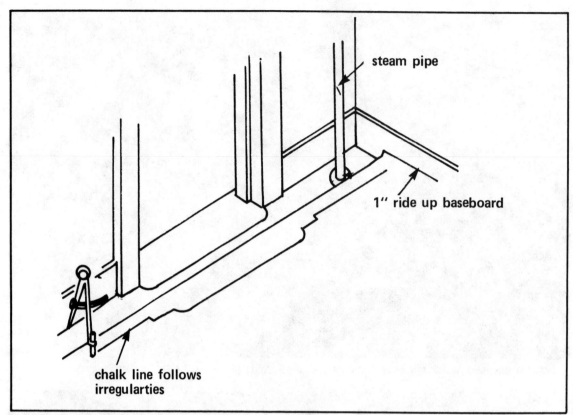

steam pipe

1" ride up baseboard

chalk line follows
irregularties

Fig. 3-20. Scribing a wall line for installing sheet flooring.

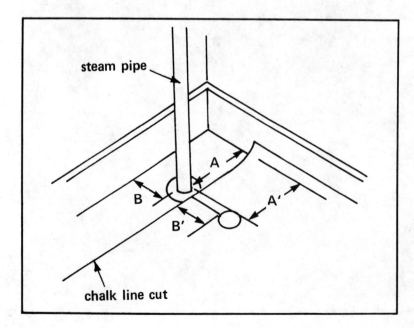

steam pipe

A

B

A'

B'

chalk line cut

Fig. 3-21. Fitting sheet flooring
around a pipe.

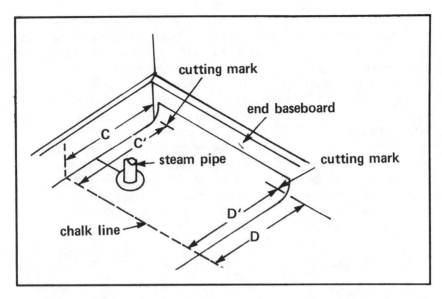

Fig. 3-22. Scribing the end wall line.

the pipe. Move the flooring against the wall and around the pipe to test the fit. Trim if necessary.

Next, fit the ends of the sheet to the end baseboards. If the baseboard is straight and even, draw a chalk line parallel to the end wall across the flooring sheet, up the baseboard, and across the floor, as shown in Fig. 322. The line should be 1 to 2 feet from the end of the sheet. Measure the distance (C) from the wall to the chalk line on the baseboard and transfer to the flooring (C'). Use a flexible metal tape rule for accurate measurement on the sheet. Measure the distance (D) from the

Fig. 3-23. Cutting the second sheet of flooring.

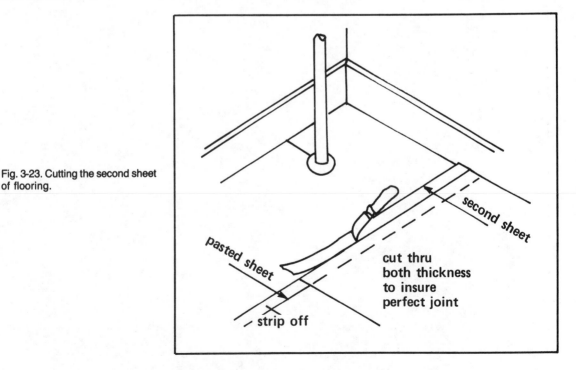

wall to the chalked line on the floor and transfer to the flooring (D'). Draw a line between the two cutting marks and cut along the line.

To paste the flooring down, fold back one end of the sheet until it meets the other end. Spread the mastic or adhesive on the exposed felt or the subfloor. Replace the flooring over the adhesive on the exposed floor, then replace the other end of the sheet.

To finish your sheet flooring job, cut the second piece 2 inches longer than the room, as described in Fig. 3-23. Then lay the piece over the first piece with a 1-inch overlap. Set dividers to that the legs are 1/2 inch apart. Set the sharp point at the edge of the second sheet and scribe a line the length of the sheet. Holding a linoleum knife at exactly right angles to the material, cut through the new sheet onto the undersheet, leaving the guideline for the cut on the pasted sheet. Now cut along the line on the pasted sheet. Test the two new edges; they should butt exactly. Finally, paste the second sheet the same way as the first.

When the flooring is completely fitted and pasted, roll thoroughly with a flooring roller or rolling pin. Wait 24 hours, then wash thoroughly. Finally, replace the moldings. For most do-it-yourselfers, resilient tile floors are easier to install and trim than larger sheet flooring.

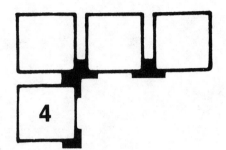

Installing Hard Tile Floors

Tile has been used for hundreds of years because it is one of the most durable and easy to care for building materials. This practical tradition is being carried on today as the fashionable way to decorate your home—and not just in the kitchen or bath. Ceramic, mosaic, and quarry tiles are being installed throughout the home—in entryways, under woodstoves, and in hallways, bedrooms, kitchens, dining areas, dens, studies, and other rooms. Hard tiles offer a look of permanence.

Floor tiles can be laid on any solid surface as long as the base is firm and even. Exterior plywood can be laid over a subflooring to form an excellent base for a long-lasting tile floor. Exterior plywood includes water-resistant glues that interior plywood doesn't have. Floor tiles can also be laid over an old linoleum or vinyl sheet flooring as long as the surface is clean, flat, and will accept the adhesive used.

INSTALLING CERAMIC MOSAIC TILE

A popular and easy type of floor tile to install is the *ceramic mosaic*. It is a baked tile, smaller in size then common tile, and often manufactured in sheets held together by a fabric backing. This backing offers correct spacing for the grout to be applied later. Let's take a look at the installation of this ceramic mosaic tile one step at a time.

Figure 4-1 illustrates how the sheets of ceramic mosaic tile are laid out on an older floor in order to decide on the correct spacing. The floor has been repaired as needed and checked for a smooth surface. If the floor were rough, it would have to be removed using techniques outlined in Chapter 3.

Once the ceramic mosaic sheets have been laid out, you must mark out a centerline for the room so that all sheets will be squared as they are installed. Find the centers of two sidewalls and draw a line between them using a straightedge (Fig. 4-2).

Make sure that the old floor has a good surface. Abrade the existing floor to remove wax and produce a better surface so that the adhesive will stick to the floor (Fig. 4-3).

The adhesive is prepared next. In this case, the

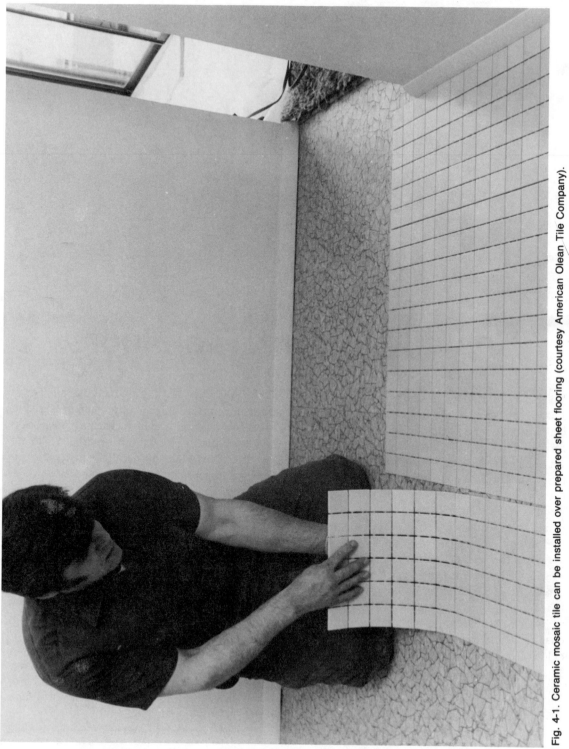

Fig. 4-1. Ceramic mosaic tile can be installed over prepared sheet flooring (courtesy American Olean Tile Company).

Fig. 4-2. Drawing the line from which sheets of ceramic mosaic tile will be installed (courtesy American Olean Tile Company).

do-it-yourselfer is using a three-part epoxy (Fig. 4-4). It includes the epoxy resin, the hardener, and a mortar mix. They are mixed together in a bucket with an electric mixer or by hand with a clean wooden paddle. It should be smooth, trowelable, and lump-free. Don't mix more mortar than can be used in about 1/2 hour because it will set up hard to use after that time.

Next, apply the mortar (Fig. 4-5). Spread the epoxy with a 1/8- × -1/8- × -1/8-inch notched trowel recommended for setting ceramic mosaics. Other adhesives will have other specifics. Use the flat edge of the trowel to lay down the mortar and use the notched edge to smooth it out to the correct thickness.

You're now ready to install the first sheet of ceramic mosaics (Fig. 4-6). Lay it carefully, making sure that the top edge matches the line drawn on the floor and the wall. Also make sure that there is not an excess or a lack of mortar under the tile sheets.

Sheets may have to be cut in order to fit. Figure 4-7 illustrates how a tile saw is used to cut ceramic mosaic sheets. You can also use a tile snapper and glass cutter, however, as described in Chapter 2. Figure 4-8 shows the scoring and braking of ceramic mosaic tile sheets with such a cutter. Make sure that sheets of plastic have been placed over any surface you don't want to clean later. Tile dust is very find and difficult to remove from rugs and fabric surfaces.

Once in place over the mortar, the tile is seated firmly with a beating block (Fig. 4-9). Make sure that the block is large enough to disperse pressure. Otherwise, a tile could be chipped or cracked, making it necessary for you to remove the sheet or make a repair to the individual tile.

Next comes the fun part: waiting. Depending upon the type of adhesive used, you may have to wait 12 to 48 hours so that the mortar will cure before you add the grouting. Chapter 2 offers information and a table to guide you in the selection of ceramic mosaic tile grouting.

Once the grout is mixed, it is spread over a small area on the surface of the ceramic mosaic tiles (Fig. 4-10). This allows the grout to be worked into the space between the tiles, minimizing gaps and air spaces. The grout is spread with a rubber-facet grouting trowel designed especially for the job. A hard metal trowel would scratch the surface of the tiles and not control the grouting of convex-shaped tiles.

When you're done, sprinkle dry grout over the surface (Fig. 4-11). Then rub the grouted surface of the tile with burlap to compact the joints and force out any entrapped air (Fig. 4-12).

All finished! Figure 4-13 shows the completed porcelain ceramic mosaic floor. The same tile is shown on the counter and backsplash. The cement grout joints may be treated with a silicone sealer or lemon furniture oil to prevent food stains.

Sometimes the surface you tile with ceramic tile is not flat. It may be stair-stepped or require a cove base. Figures 4-14 through 4-18 illustrate the installation of such tiles on stairs, at doorways, and walls.

INSTALLING CERAMIC TILE

Ceramic tile is larger than ceramic mosaic and doesn't have the mesh bonding to evenly space tiles; so it requires more skill to install. The following instructions, however, offer easy-to-follow steps for even the first-time do-it-yourselfer. The instructions specifically describe the installation of ceramic tile, but are equally valuable in the laying of a quarry tile or paver floor.

The example was installed in a new greenhouse built onto a 50-year-old home made of granite rock (Fig. 4-19). The ceramic tile was chosen both as a complementary decoration and as a practical heat sink to help collect and retain heat in the greenhouse. The existing patio was reinforced and then leveled with a 4-inch mortar bed.

The first step was to thoroughly clean the concrete slab. There are a variety of products available for this task through your tile retailer. If you are building over a wood subfloor, make sure that the surface is clean and flat. Refer to Fig. 4-20.

To square off the room, lines are drawn across the width and length through the center point of the room (Fig. 4-21). Parallel lines are then drawn

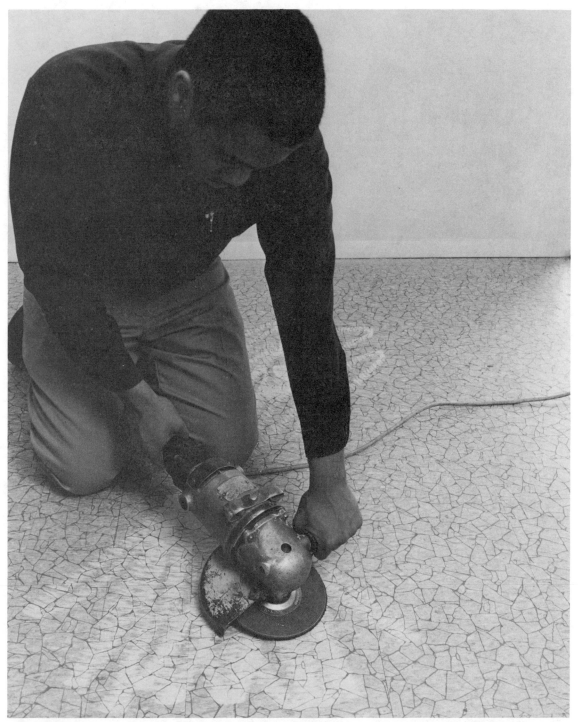

Fig. 4-3. Abrading the existing vinyl floor to remove wax and provide for better adhesion (courtesy American Olean Tile Company).

Fig. 4-4. Mixing three-part epoxy adhesive (courtesy American Olean Tile Company).

Fig. 4-5. Spreading epoxy adhesive with notched trowel (courtesy American Olean Tile Company).

Fig. 4-6. Installing sheets of ceramic mosaic tile (courtesy American Olean Tile Company).

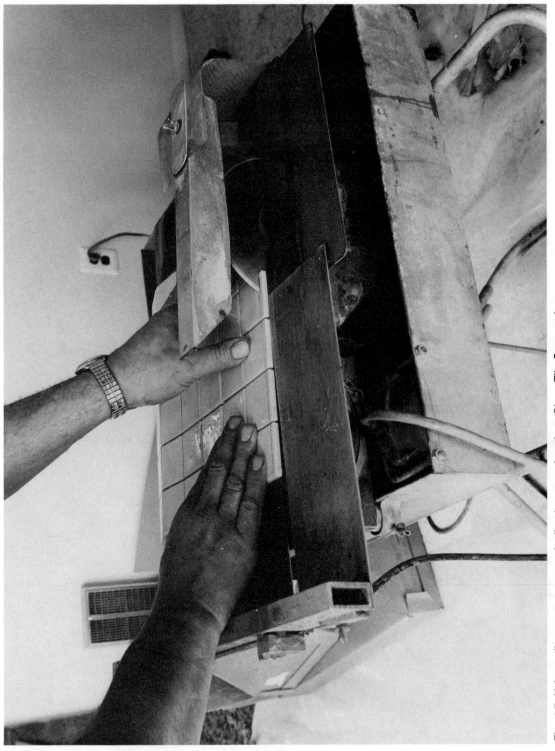

Fig. 4-7. Using a tile saw to cut ceramic tiles (courtesy American Olean Tile Company).

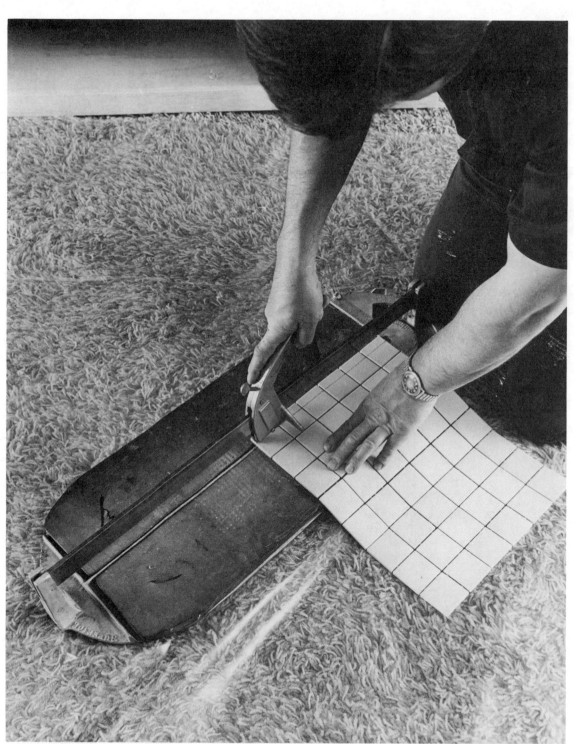

Fig. 4-8. Using a tile cutter (courtesy American Olean Tile Company).

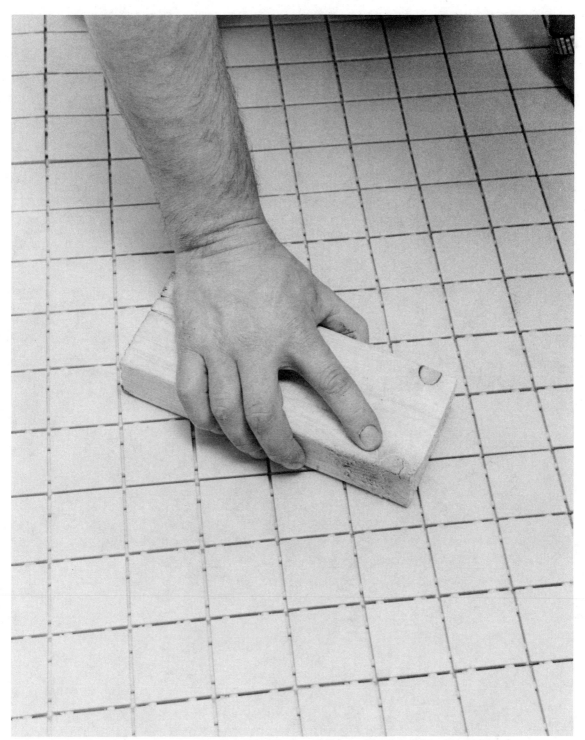

Fig. 4-9. Using a beating block to set tile firmly into the epoxy (courtesy American Olean Tile Company).

Fig. 4-10. Spreading grout over the tile with a rubber-faced grout trowel (courtesy American Olean Tile Company).

Fig. 4-11. Sprinkle dry grout over the surface (courtesy American Olean Tile Company).

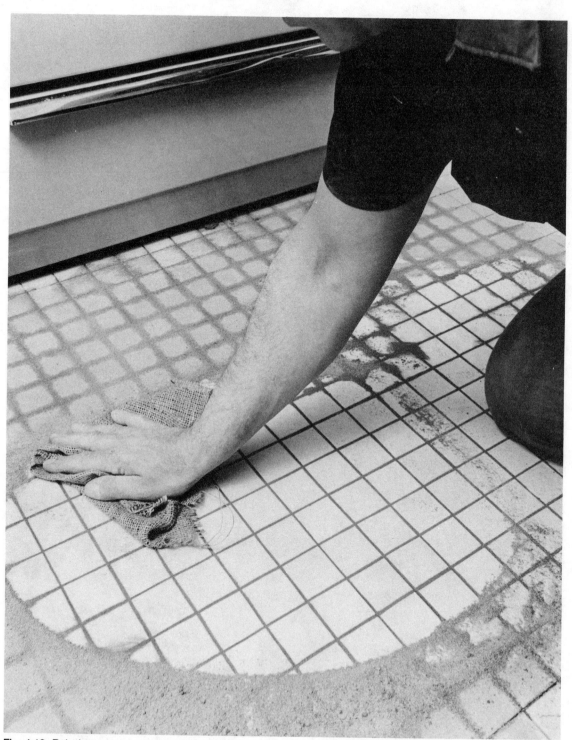

Fig. 4-12. Rub the grouted surface with a burlap cloth (courtesy American Olean Tile Company).

Fig. 4-13. The finished porcelain ceramic mosaic floor (courtesy American Olean Tile Company).

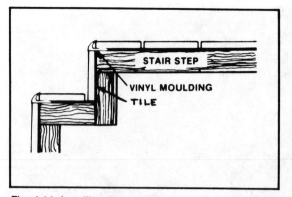

Fig. 4-14. Installing tiles along stairs (courtesy Color Tile Supermart).

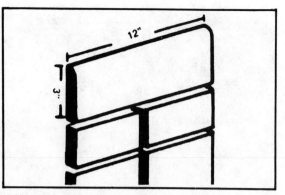

Fig. 4-17. Installing tile at a doorway (courtesy Color Tile Supermart).

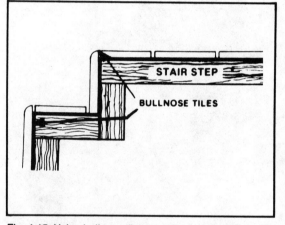

Fig. 4-15. Using bullnose tiles on stairs (courtesy Color Tile Supermart).

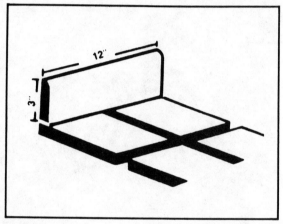

Fig. 4-18. Installing a cove base tile (courtesy Color Tile Supermart).

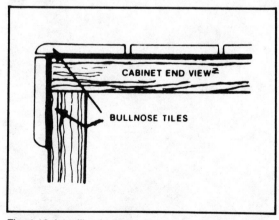

Fig. 4-16. Installing bullnose tiles on the edge of a cabinet (courtesy Color Tile Supermart).

as guidelines to ensure that the square tiles will be symmetrical with the square room.

Layout of the tile begins at the exterior edge of the greenhouse where tiles will be installed. Any necessary cuts can then be made along the interior wall where they are less visible. Using two straightedges and a square edge, the starting lines are first established (Fig. 4-22). To begin, the position of the first three rows is established by placing a square edge against the line and a straightedge, as shown in Fig. 4-23.

Every effort is made at the tile factories to ensure consistent color. The clay and the baking process, however, bring in variables that often make tiles slightly different in tint. To disperse the color

Fig. 4-19. Newly added greenhouse anticipating the installation of a ceramic tile floor (courtesy American Olean Tile Company).

Fig. 4-20. Beginning installation with a thoroughly cleaned concrete slab (courtesy American Olean Tile Company).

Fig. 4-21. Drawing guidelines (courtesy American Olean Tile Company).

Fig. 4-22. Beginning at the exterior edge of the greenhouse floor (courtesy American Olean Tile Company).

Fig. 4-23. Position the first three rows (courtesy American Olean Tile Company).

variations throughout the floor and make a more beautiful design, shuffle the tiles before installation (Fig. 4-24). Select tile from three boxes, making sure the batch number is the same, and shuffle the tile for a thorough mix.

The next step is to mix the adhesive mortar (Fig. 4-25). There are various mortars and floor mixes available. Use the one recommended for your specific type and installation. This mix includes latex additives to accommodate expansion and contraction.

Using the smooth side of a 1/4-×-3/8-×-1/4-inch notched trowel, spread the floor mix in a small area (Fig. 4-26). Comb the mortar with the notched edge of the trowel to ensure even distribution of mortar. A row of tile is installed against the straightedge, which has been placed along guidelines. Many do-it-yourselfers purchase and use spacers (Fig. 4-27) to make sure that the tiles are evenly spaced.

Once the first row is in, additional rows are set, lining up the joints (Fig. 4-28). After the first three rows are laid, a wooden block is used to beat the tile flat into the mortar to ensure a good bond (Fig. 4-29).

Periodically remove one tile to check the bond (Fig. 4-30). Mortar must evenly cover the back of the tile and bond with the concrete slab. This is crucial, especially in a passive solar design, because air pockets would not permit efficient conduction of the sun's heat through to the mortar bed for storage.

The next section of tile is set in a similar manner using the straightedge for the six throw and filling in the next two rows. Check frequently with the square edge to be sure joints are lined up (Fig. 4-31).

When coming to the inside wall, partial tiles have to be installed (Fig. 4-32). Cuts are made with a tile cutter (Fig. 4-33), as explained in Chapter 2. Sometimes a special cut must be made in a tile to fit around an obstacle, such as a rock in a wall (Fig. 4-34). This cut is made with tile nippers.

Finally, the floor tiles are set (Fig. 4-35). Depending on the mortar used and local weather conditions, you should wait 3 or 4 days to allow the flooring to cure before grout is installed. Grouting too soon could cause tile to shift and make repair difficult.

Grouting should be selected based upon the type of tile, the type of installation, and the manufacturer's and dealer's recommendations. The grout should be mixed thoroughly (Fig. 4-36). Check to see that there is no powder at the bottom. Scrape off the sides of the bucket. The grout should be the consistency of marshmallow fluff. Let it set up for a few minutes, then remix.

Once the tile has set up and you are sure it won't shift when walked upon, mix up the grout and spread it on (Fig. 4-37). Using a rubber-faced grouting trowel, spread the grout to fill the joints between the tiles. When you're done, scrape excess grout away along the edges (Figs. 4-38 and 4-39) using a putty knife.

Next, sprinkle dry grout mix over the tile surface to absorb moisture in the joints until the joints appear dark and moist (Fig. 4-40). Using a clean, dry cloth, rub the tile surface in a circular motion to loosen excess grout and to compact the joints (Fig. 4-41). Allow the floor to stand for at least 15 minutes.

Using a damp Turkish towel, wipe the tile surface to clean off the excess grout (Fig. 4-42). Rinse the towel and change the water frequently (Fig. 4-43). Repeat wiping until the tile appears clean (Fig. 4-44). A slight film will develop on the tile as the floor dries.

It's time to step back and take a look (Fig. 4-45). Notice the even shading of the tile and the flat, compact joints in the grouted floor.

Again, you should give your new floor a few days to dry out before cleaning up. Final cleanup can be done using concrete and masonry cleaner (Fig. 4-46). The cleaner contains acids and wetting agents for the removal of acids, stains, and mortar deposits.

Scrub the tile surface briskly with a brush and the solution (Fig. 4-47). This cleaner will not stain metal and may be applied to a dry floor. The long-handled brush keeps splatters away from your skin. Rubber gloves are recommended. Allow the solution to stand on the tile for 7 to 8 minutes for best results.

Fig. 4-24. Shuffle tiles before installation (courtesy American Olean Tile Company).

Fig. 4-25. Mix the adhesive mortar (courtesy American Olean Tile Company).

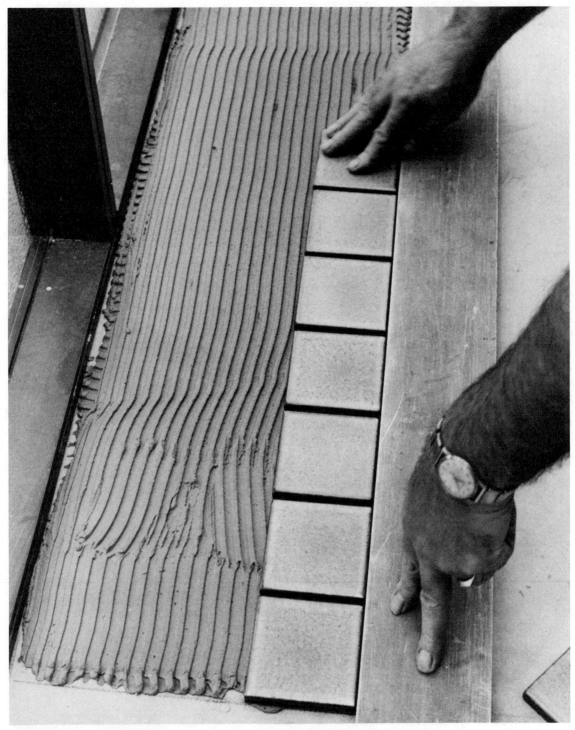

Fig. 4-26. Spread the floor mix in a small area (courtesy American Olean Tile Company).

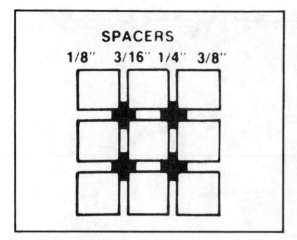

Fig. 4-27. Installing spacers between tiles (courtesy Color Tile Supermart).

Finally, flood the area with clean water using a large sponge (Fig. 4-48). Then drag a towel through puddles to life off the solution and grout (Fig. 4-49). Squeeze the saturated towel into a bucket. Repeat the process for the final rinse (Fig. 4-50). Flood the floor with clear water and wipe dry, dragging the towel and wringing it dry to remove all water from the floor. The tile is now clean and sparkling with no trace of grout or streaks (Fig. 4-51).

Figure 4-52 illustrates how the new ceramic tile floor bends in with the rest of the house. The living room extends under the sun. Ceramic tile warms the floor of this passive solar glass-enclosed porch by conducting the sun's heat into the cement slab below. Shady leaves from the backyard tree

Fig. 4-28. Spacing between tiles can also be done with a straightedge and your eyes (courtesy American Olean Tile Company).

Fig. 4-29. Beat the tile with a wooden block to ensure good bond (courtesy American Olean Tile Company).

Fig. 4-30. Remove one tile to check bond (courtesy American Olean Tile Company).

Fig. 4-31. Set the next section of tile (courtesy American Olean Tile Company).

Fig. 4-32. Installing partial tiles at the inside wall (courtesy American Olean Tile Company).

keep it cool in the summer. Screen windows and door add ventilation. The sunroom also opens to an outdoor patio.

Sometimes a floor will extend on to a nearby wall with tile making the transition. This is especially popular in the bathroom where a ceramic tile floor blends into a ceramic tile shower. Figures 4-53 through 4-57 illustrate how this can be easily accomplished by the do-it-yourselfer.

INSTALLING QUARRY TILE

Quarry tile can add the perfect touch of sophistication to your home and offers a lifetime floor covering to any room. Its durable composition can handle heavy traffic areas.

Preparation and installation techniques are, for the most part, very similar to those for other types of ceramic tile. Refer to earlier illustrations as the steps for installing quarry tile are offered.

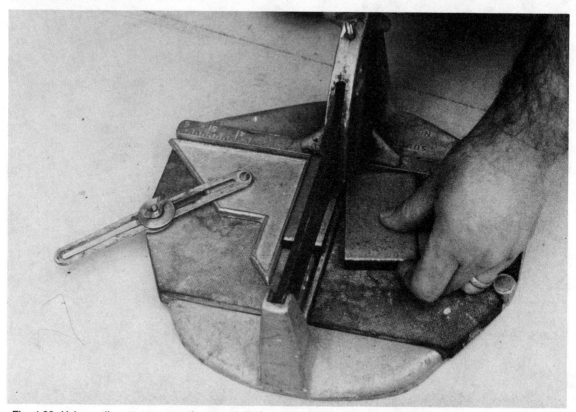

Fig. 4-33. Using a tile cutter to snap the scored tile (courtesy American Olean Tile Company).

Fig. 4-34. Special cut to fit rough outline on rock wall (courtesy American Olean Tile Company).

First, prepare the subfloor surface as you would for ceramic tile according to the type of adhesive you will be using and the manufacturer's directions for that adhesive. Next, establish working lines are you would for ceramic tile.

Most of the tools and suppliers used for ceramic tile installation can be used for quarry tile installation as well—trowels, cutters, nippers, spacers, etc. Assemble all tools and supplies. Make sure all cartons of tiles are uniform and tiles are in acceptable condition.

To set quarry tile, first mix the adhesive according to the manufacturer's directions. Apply the adhesive to the subfloor with a notched trowel.

Work only one quadrant at a time.

Next, set all whole tiles first, using the pyramid sequence described earlier. Quarry tiles generally have wider joints then ceramic tiles. To achieve a wider, even joint, you can do one of two things: add spacers between each tile to achieve uniform spacing or use a line gauge which automatically measures and establishes spacing between quarry tiles. Make sure all lines and joints are straight and uniform. Then remove excess adhesive from the tile while the adhesive is still wet.

Set the remaining quadrants in the same manner. Then measure and cut quarry border tiles as you would ceramic border tiles. Allow the adhesive

Fig. 4-35. Tile floor is set. Wait 3 or 4 days for curing (courtesy American Olean Tile Company).

Fig. 4-36. Mix grout thoroughly (courtesy American Olean Tile Company).

Fig. 4-37. Spreading grout with a grout trowel (courtesy American Olean Tile Company).

Fig. 4-38. Scrap excess grout from the edge (courtesy American Olean Tile Company).

Fig. 4-39. Removing grout from entryway (courtesy American Olean Tile Company).

Fig. 4-40. Sprinkle dry grout over the tile surface (courtesy American Olean Tile Company).

Fig. 4-41. Rub tile to loosen excess grout and compact joints (courtesy American Olean Tile Company).

Fig. 4-42. Wipe tile surface with damp towel (courtesy American Olean Tile Company).

Fig. 4-43. Rinse towel and change water frequently (courtesy American Olean Tile Company).

130

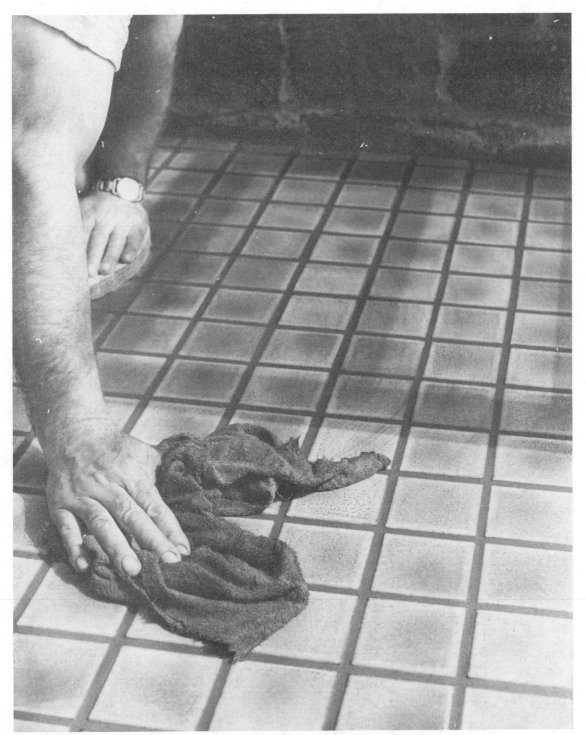

Fig. 4-44. Repeat wiping until the tile appears clean (courtesy American Olean Tile Company).

Fig. 4-45. Inspecting the cleaned tile floor (courtesy American Olean Tile Company).

Fig. 4-46. Concrete and masonry cleaner (courtesy American Olean Tile Company).

Fig. 4-47. Scrub the tile surface briskly with brush and solution (courtesy American Olean Tile Company).

Fig. 4-48. Flood the area with clean water using a large sponge (courtesy American Olean Tile Company).

Fig. 4-49. Drag a towel through puddles to lift off the solution and grout (courtesy American Olean Tile Company).

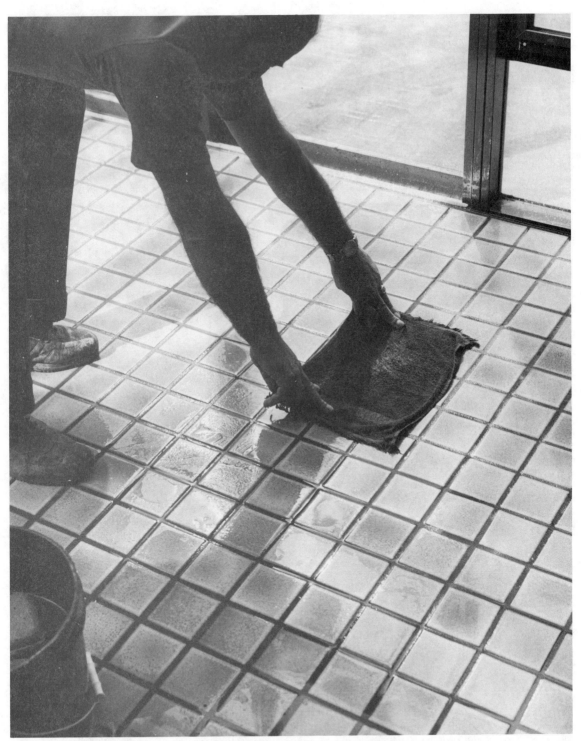

Fig. 4-50. Repeat the process for the final rinse (courtesy American Olean Tile Company).

Fig. 4-51. Cleaned and sparkling tile floor (courtesy American Olean Tile Company).

Fig. 4-52. The finished greenhouse room (courtesy American Olean Tile Company).

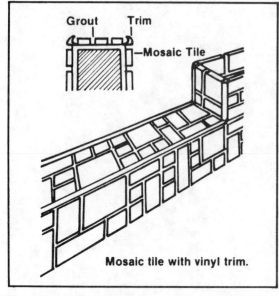

Mosaic tile with vinyl trim.

Fig. 4-53. Installing mosaic tile on the shower sill and jamb (courtesy Color Tile Supermart).

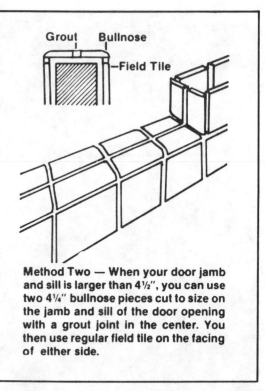

Method Two — When your door jamb and sill is larger than 4½", you can use two 4¼" bullnose pieces cut to size on the jamb and sill of the door opening with a grout joint in the center. You then use regular field tile on the facing of either side.

Fig. 4-55. An alternate method of installing ceramic tile on the shower sill and jamb (courtesy Color Tile Supermart).

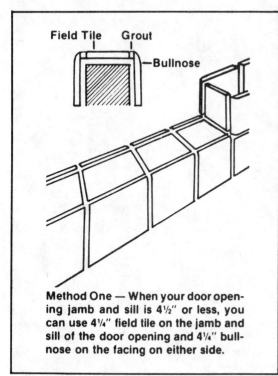

Method One — When your door opening jamb and sill is 4½" or less, you can use 4¼" field tile on the jamb and sill of the door opening and 4¼" bullnose on the facing on either side.

Fig. 4-54. Installing ceramic tile on the shower sill and jamb (courtesy Color Tile Supermart).

to dry 24 hours before grouting.

For unglazed quarry tile use a recommended grout release. Mix the grout according to the manufacturer's directions, then apply the grout to the tile surface with a rubber-faced trowel. Work thoroughly into joints. Sponge excess grout off tiles with a damp sponge.

Remove the film by buffing with a dry, soft cleaning pad. Caulk and seal the grouted surface after the grout is completely cured, usually 72 hours to 2 weeks. Buff the sealed surface with a clean rag.

INSTALLING MOLDINGS

Once your hard tile floor is finished, you can add the wood trim, or molding, around the circumference of the room. Base molding serves as the finish between the finished floor and the wall. It is available in several widths and forms. Two-piece base consists of a baseboard topped with a

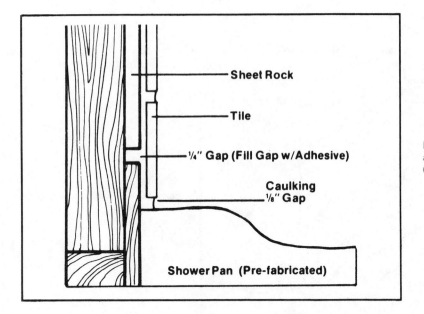

Sheet Rock

Tile

¼" Gap (Fill Gap w/Adhesive)

Caulking
⅛" Gap

Shower Pan (Pre-fabricated)

Fig. 4-56. Tile installation around a prefabricated shower pan (courtesy Color Tile Supermart).

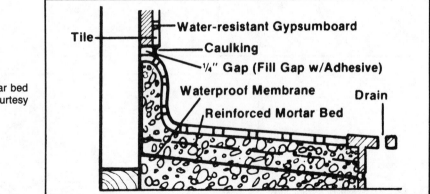

Tile

Water-resistant Gypsumboard

Caulking

¼" Gap (Fill Gap w/Adhesive)

Waterproof Membrane

Drain

Reinforced Mortar Bed

Fig. 4-57. Reinforced mortar bed shower pan installation (courtesy Color Tile Supermart).

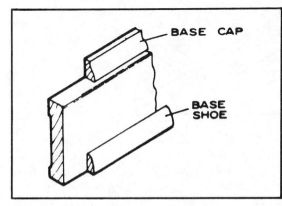

BASE CAP

BASE SHOE

Fig. 4-58. Base molding and small base cap.

Fig. 4-59. Small and large one-piece base moldings.

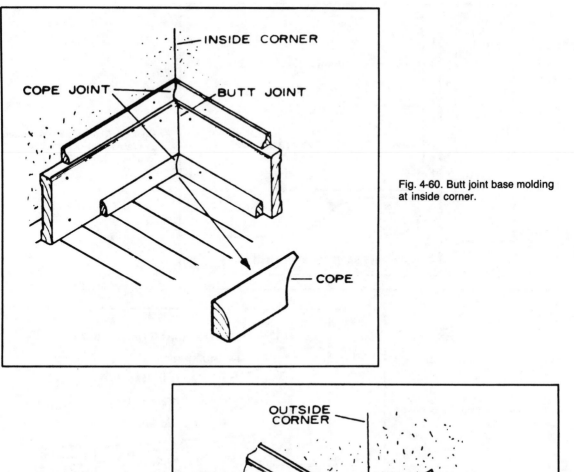

Fig. 4-60. Butt joint base molding at inside corner.

Fig. 4-61. Milter joint base molding at outside corner.

small base cap (Fig. 4-58). When the wall is not straight and true, the small base molding will conform more closely to the variations than will the wider base alone. A common size for this type of baseboard is 5/8 × 3 1/4 inches and wider (Fig. 4-59). Although a wood member is desirable at the junction of the wall and floor to serve as a protective "bumper," wood trim is sometimes eliminated entirely. Most baseboards are finished with a base shoe, 1/2 × 1/4 inch in size, as shown in Figs. 4-58 and 4-59.

Square-edge baseboard should be installed with

a butt joint at inside corners (Fig. 4-60) and a mitered joint at outside corners (Fig. 4-61). It should be nailed to each stud with two 8d (eight-penny) finishing nails. Molded single-piece bases, base moldings, and base shoes have a coped joint at inside corners and a mitered joint at outside corners. A *coped joint* is one in which the first piece is square-cut against the wall or base, and the second molding coped. This is done by sawing a 45-degree miter cut and, with a coping saw, trimming the molding along the inner line of the miter (Fig. 4-61).

The base shoe should be nailed into the flooring with long, slender nails and not into the baseboard itself. Thus, if there is a small amount of shrinkage of the joists, no opening will occur under the shoe.

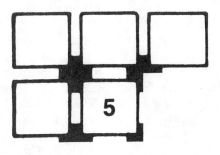

5

Maintaining Tile Floors

Proper care and protection will keep your resilient or hard tile floor looking beautiful and performing its best. Just how much attention it needs will depend on the type of floor you buy and on how much traffic it gets every day.

All floor coverings need to be washed on a regular basis to keep them clean and presentable. Floor washing techniques will be covered later. Keeping your floor looking its best also requires preventive care to avoid gouges, stains, scratches, chips, etc.

PREVENTION FOR RESILIENT FLOORS

Only a few minutes of daily care can go a long way toward helping your resilient floor stay looking its best. Here are a few tips to help you decide what to do and when.

If you've just installed a new vinyl floor, damp mop it immediately. Don't scrub or wash your new floor, though, for at least another 5 days.

When moving heavy furniture or appliances, use plywood or hardboard panels and "walk" the furniture or appliance across the panel. Another way is to slip a scrap of carpet or rub face down under each leg and slide the furniture carefully to avoid scratching or gouging.

Be careful! Some carpet dyes can "walk off" and permanently stain resilient flooring. Ask your flooring retainer about the color fastness of your carpeting. Asphalt compounds, like driveway sealers, can also permanently stain resilient flooring. Place mats or throw rugs near outside doors to keep asphalt, dirt, and moisture from being tracked in. Some rubber-backed mats can cause the floor to discolor in time; so it's best to use a mat or rug that doesn't have a rubber or latex backing.

Sweep, dust-mop, or vacuum your floor daily to remove loose dirt before it can scratch your floor's surface. Wipe up wet spills as soon as possible before they dry. Remove dried spills with a damp cloth or mop.

Use floor protectors on legs of furniture to minimize scratches and indentations. Floor protectors are available from your flooring retailer and at most hardware stores.

Roller-type casters on furniture may damage resilient flooring. Be certain that caster wheels or glides have a flat surface contact with your floor. If not, change them or place floor protectors under them.

CARING FOR NO-WAX FLOORS

No-wax floor tiles have become popular in the home furnishings market in the last few years because they do not need to be scrubbed or/and waxed. The no-wax tiles have a special wear and gloss layer that shines without waxing.

No-wax doesn't mean no-care, however. Although the new no-wax floors are bright, shiny, and easier to clean than regular vinyl floor tiles, they still require cleaning. This is true of any surface in the home, especially one that takes the abuse and pounding that a floor receives. Here are some suggestions that will help you maintain the sparkling appearance of your no-wax tile floors (Figs. 5-1 and 5-2).

To clean, sweep or vacuum your floor to remove loose dirt. Floors that are lightly soiled will require mopping or sponging with clean water to help remove the dirt.

Since no-wax tile surfaces tend to hide dirt, the floor should be washed regularly with a mild household detergent. Don't use soap-based cleaners because they can leave a dulling film.

Using a mop or sponge, apply the detergent to a small area of the floor. Enough pressure on the mop or sponge will help clean the embossed design on the tile surface. For stubborn dirt, use the nylon cleaning pad on the mop, but don't use abrasive pads such as steel wool or scouring pads. Rinse the floor thoroughly with clean warm water to prevent dirty water from remaining on the embossed areas. Remember, no-wax tile floors do not require buffing.

In areas that are used constantly, heavy foot traffic could begin to reduce some of the surface gloss on a no-wax floor. To restore luster, use a no-wax floor finish after cleaning the floor, allowing it to completely dry. If you decide to apply a second coat, do so after the first is completely dry.

No-wax floors can be damaged by intense heat and lighted cigarettes, as well as rubber- or foam-backed mats or rugs. Avoid applying carnauba or water waxes and vinyl dressings because they will not adhere and will create a dull film, or haze, on your floor.

Commonly used household products can stain your no-wax floor and should be wiped up immediately with an absorbent paper towel or cloth and washed with a full-strength detergent. If this doesn't do the job, try rubbing with alcohol or lighter fluid. Spills from certain products can be cleaned by following these instructions:

☐ Iodine, mustard, mercurochrome, merthiolate, and certain ink spills should be wiped up with an absorbent paper towel or cloth. Remove the stain by dampening a clean cloth with rubbing alcohol and wiping over the surface. Wait 30 minutes before walking on the area.

☐ Asphalt, inks, shoe polish, and tar stains can be removed by rubbing a dampened cloth with lighter fluid over the stained areas.

☐ Remove paint stains and varnishes by wiping a damp cloth with turpentine or thinner over the spill. Never use paint remover on a no-wax floor tile.

CARING FOR VINYL FLOORS

Resilient vinyl floor tile requires more care than no-wax flooring, but can still be easy to maintain (Figs. 5-3 and 5-4).

Wash the floor with a cleaning solution made according to the label instructions on a general-purpose liquid detergent. Ideally, you should use one sponge mop and bucket to wash the floor and another mop and bucket to rinse. If you use only one mop, no matter how much you wring it out, you won't get all the detergent out of the sponge and a dulling film will be left on your floor.

Dip your sponge mop into the cleaning solution, and without wringing it out, spread the cleaning

Fig. 5-1. No-wax tile floors can be maintained with a minimum of effort (courtesy Azrock Floor Products).

Fig. 5-2. Today's tile floors can keep a sheen much longer than waxed linoleum (courtesy Azrock Floor Products).

Fig. 5-3. Resilient vinyl composition tile floor (courtesy Azrock Floor Products).

solution on a small area of the floor—about 3 × 3 feet. Relax for a minute and let the cleaning solution do the work for you. The detergent action will loosen a lot of the dirt and keep it suspended for easy pickup.

Now go over the area again with the sponge mop, scrubbing hard enough to loosen the remaining dirt. If you have a mop with a nylon scrubbing pad, you can get up hard-to-remove marks with the nylon pad.

Wring out the sponge mop thoroughly and take up the cleaning solution left on the floor. Then take a second bucket of clean warm water and a rinse-only mop and rinse thoroughly. Often, general-purpose detergent directions will say rinsing is not necessary. While this may be true on other surfaces, it's not true on floors. Any detergent film left on a floor will hold tracked-in dirt and dull the surface.

Repeat this procedure of washing and rinsing one area at a time until the whole floor is clean. Change rinse water often to make sure you're not redepositing any dirt or detergent. Allow the floor to dry thoroughly before using. If you intend to apply a protective floor polish on the same day, make sure your floor is completely dry before applying.

A word of caution: never use steel wool or scouring cleaners on vinyl floor tile. For heavily soiled or exceptionally dirty areas of the floor, thoroughly clean with a full-strength cleaner designed for your specific floor. Allow the cleaner to soak in a few minutes, then use a nylon pad or scrub brush to loosen dirt.

APPLYING FLOOR POLISH

Here's how to apply floor polish to your vinyl or similar tile floor. First, wash the floor thoroughly. Then allow the floor to dry at least 20 to 30 minutes.

Apply the polish in a thin uniform coat. Do not use a sponge mop that has been used previously to clean the floor. There always will be some detergent film in the sponge, which can cause streaking and clouding of the polish.

To apply a thin coat, pour the floor polish directly onto the applicator, or put the polish in a bucket, dip the mop, and wring it out gently. When applying, move the applicator in all directions to ensure even distribution. Don't rub the applicator too vigorously since this can cause bubbles.

When multiple coats of polish are to be applied, wait at least 30 minutes between each application. Make sure you follow specific drying instructions on the polish container. Allow to dry completely before using the room.

REMOVING FLOOR POLISH

Stripping removes the successive layers of polish and dirt. The best way to tell whether your floor needs stripping is to *test-strip* a small, out-of-the-way area. Compare the results against the surrounding area. If the rest of the floor has noticeably less pattern and color clarity, chances are that stripping and repolishing are needed.

First, sweep or vacuum the floor thoroughly. Apply a liberal amount of a good wax or polish remover over a 3- × -3-foot area with a sponge mop. Allow the solution to stand 3 to 5 minutes so it can soak in and soften the polish.

Next use a sponge mop, nonwoven pad, scrub brush, or electric floor scrubber with nonabrasive pads to loosen the old polish film. Pick up the cleaning solution and old polish with a sponge mop or cloth. Rinse the floor with warm water and a clean sponge mop. If some film remains from the old polish, repeat the stripping operation where needed, then rinse.

Repeat the procedure area by area until the entire floor is stripped. Let the floor dry. It should look dull but clean and is now ready for polishing, as just outlined.

CARING FOR LINOLEUM

While most resilient floors installed today are vinyl or no-wax, there are still many thousands of homes that have long-lasting linoleum flooring. Specific instructions on how to maintain linoleum flooring follow.

Linoleum, whether for floor coverings, kitchen countertops, walls, or other inside surfaces, will stay attractive longer and wear better if waxed and polished. A few simple rules for its care will be found useful:

Fig. 5-4. Vinyl tile is often used in high-traffic businesses due to ease of maintenance (courtesy Azrock Floor Products).

- ☐ Dust daily.
- ☐ Use water sparingly.
- ☐ Clean with special mild linoleum cleaner, soap, or mild detergent solution.
- ☐ Apply was in a thin, even film.
- ☐ Rewax only as needed, usually no more than once a month.
- ☐ Never use harsh abrasives other than fine steel wool to take off spots that are hard to remove.

No matter what type of wax is used, always start with a clean surface before waxing. There are some excellent linoleum cleaners which may be diluted with water in accordance with the manufacturer's directions. In using them, clean only a few square feet at a time, going over that area with a fresh cloth wrung out with clear, lukewarm water. Permit the surface to dry thoroughly and the wax to spread evenly.

Waxes that protect linoleum are essentially of two types: paste and liquid waxes with a volatile-solvent base and self-polishing waxes with a water-emulsion base. They should be applied in very thin coats to avoid making the floor slippery.

Volatile-solvent waxes may be obtained in either paste or liquid form. The liquid is somewhat easier to apply than the paste because of the large proportion of solvent. Both paste and liquid are suitable for linoleum, as well as for other types of floor surfaces.

Paste wax should be applied with a slightly dampened soft cloth or with a wax applicator and allowed to dry, after which it should be polished to a lustrous finish. Liquid wax should be spread evenly over the cleaned surface with a lamb's wool applicator in straight, parallel strokes. After drying for 30 minutes, it should be polished to a lustrous finish. Waxes of the organic-solvent type must not be used on asphalt tile because they soften and mar the surface of the tile.

Self-polishing or water-emulsion base waxes will give a protective coating if used on linoleum, rubber tile, cork, asphalt tile, mastic, and other flooring. The wax should be spread as thinly an evenly as possible with a lamb's wool applicator or

soft cloth mop in straight, parallel strokes. If properly applied, it should dry to a hard, lustrous film in less than 30 minutes. Although not required, the gloss may be increased by a slight buffing after the wax becomes thoroughly dry.

A weighted floor brush or electric polishing machine does an efficient job with little effort. A floor polisher may be rented at a variety of retail outlets or rental yards. For a very hard surface, the linoleum should be given two or three coats of wax, making sure to let each coat dry for at least 30 minutes before polishing.

Care should be taken to not flood linoleum surfaces with water. Any water that seeps through the edges of seams may affect the cementing material and cause the backing to mildew or rot and edges of the linoleum to become loose and curled. Wiping up water as soon as it is spilled on waxed linoleum will keep light spots from appearing. Grease and other spots should be cleaned as quickly as possible with a cloth or sponge wrung out of mild lukewarm detergent solution. Rinse by using a clean cloth wrung out of clear, lukewarm water. Floor oils and sweeping compound containing oils should not be used on linoleum because these materials may leave a film of oil on the surface to collect dust and dirt.

CARING FOR ASPHALT TILE

Another flooring product commonly found in older homes is asphalt tile. Asphalt tile is often used to cover concrete and wood floors and is found in a variety of colors. Impervious to water, the tiles are especially suitable for floors on which water is likely to be spilled, such as kitchens, laundries, and bathrooms. They also provided attractive and satisfactory flooring for basement recreation rooms and enclosed porches.

Mastic floor covering of the asphalt type has asphalt, bitumen, or resin as the base and often lasts many years. Cleansers and polishes containing abrasives, oils, or organic solvents (gasoline, turpentine, carbon tetrachloride) should not be used to clean asphalt-base coverings, however. Never use unknown cleaning preparations on asphalt tile without testing them first, unless they are recommended by the manufacturer of the flooring.

To test a cleaning or polishing preparation for use on asphalt tile, moisten a white cloth with the preparation and rub over the surface of a spare tile. If the color of the tile shows on the cloth, the preparation has acted as a solvent, dissolving the surface of the tile, and is not safe to use.

Asphalt tile floors may be washed with neutral soap and lukewarm water in much the same manner as linoleum. The water will not harm the tile unless it is permitted to stand and seep under edges enough to loosen them from the floor. After cleaning and drying, the care of asphalt tile floors is similar to that recommended for linoleum with one very important exception: never use paste wax or liquid wax that has a solvent base on asphalt tiles. These waxes will soften the tile and mar the surface.

Water-emulsion or self-polishing waxes that are free from oils are suitable and safe for asphalt tile.

They should be spread as thinly as possible on the surface of the floor with lamb's-wool applicator. Use straight, parallel strokes in one direction only. In approximately 30 minutes, the wax should dry to a hard, lustrous finish. While these waxes are self-polishing to a degree, the appearance of the floor will be improved by a light buffing. Before polishing, however, the wax should be completely dry.

Wax should be renewed at intervals, depending upon the severity of wear. It is not necessary to rewax as long as the floor responds to polishing. Daily dusting and occasional machine polishing will eliminate the need of mopping and extend the life of the wax coating.

CARING FOR CERAMIC TILE

Ceramic floor and wall tile is extremely easy to care for (Figs. 5-5 through 5-9). In most cases,

Fig. 5-5. Ceramic grout and tile cleaner.

Fig. 5-6. Paver tile in a greenhouse become better solar collectors when they are properly cleaned (courtesy Tile Council of America).

deposits. Text this method in a small area first to be sure the vinegar doesn't etch your tile or erode your grout. Vinegar can damage some crystalline tile glazes.

For heavy-duty cleaning of ceramic floor and wall tile, an all-purpose cleaner should be used in areas where dirt is likely to build up. The cleaner should be applied and allowed to stand for about 5 minutes before scrubbing lightly with a brush. Hard water deposits can be removed with a commercial tile cleaner or treated with a solution of white vinegar and water in equal amounts.

Cleaning ceramic mosaic tile floors is similar. For routine cleaning, wiping with a damp sponge mop is usually the only maintenance required. You can supplement with a diluted solution of a popular household cleaner. For heavy-duty cleaning, mix a household scouring powder with water to a pastelike consistency and mop it over the floors. Allow the paste to stand for about 5 minutes. Scrub vigorously with a scrubbing brush. Rinse and wipe dry. It should be noted, however, that as ceramic mosaic floor tiles age, a patina forms on the surface. Its soft shine keeps the floor looking fresh longer and maintenance becomes easier.

Here are some notes on maintaining quarry tile floors. For routine cleaning, mop occasionally with any popular household cleaner. Rinse thoroughly to keep dull detergent film from drying on the tile surface. For heavy-duty cleaning, a thorough scrubbing with an all-purpose cleaner or scouring powder paste is recommended. Scrub vigorously using a more concentrated cleaner solution. Rinse completely. Use scouring powder for any stubborn spots which remain. Quarry tiles, too, need less maintenance as they age.

a simple wiping with a wet cloth will remove dirt and grime. More specifically, let's look at the methods of cleaning glazed and unglazed tiles, ceramic mosaics, and quarry tiles.

Glazed tiles in bathrooms and other areas are easy to routinely clean. If you have soft water, use an all-purpose cleaner on the tiles. Allow it to stand for about 5 minutes before lightly scrubbing with a sponge. Rinse well. If you have hard water, commercial tile cleaners, available at supermarkets, will do the best job. As an alternate, a solution of white vinegar and water in equal amounts should remove

REMOVING STAINS FROM HARD TILE

Here are some guides for removing stains from ceramic tile and grout.

- ☐ Blood: Use hydrogen peroxide or household bleach.
- ☐ Coffee, tea, food, fruit juices, and

Fig. 5-7. The care of entryway tile floors is especially important (courtesy Tile Council of America).

Fig. 5-8. Ceramic mosaic tile offers a hard surface that can easily be shined (courtesy Tile Council of America).

Fig. 5-9. Quarry tile was selected for beauty and ease of maintenance in this community center (courtesy Tile Council of America).

lipstick: Use popular household cleansers in hot water followed by hydrogen peroxide or household bleach. Rinse and dry.

☐ Fingernail polish: Dissolve with polish remover. If stains remain, apply liquid household bleach. Rinse and dry.

☐ Grease and fats: Use sal soda and water of Spic & Span (or equivalent) and warm water.

☐ Inks and colored dyes: Apply household bleach. Let stand until the stain disappears, keeping the surface wet. Rinse and dry.

☐ Iodine: Scrub with ammonia. Rinse and dry.

☐ Mercurochrome: Use liquid household bleach.

☐ Mildew: Use X-14 Instant Mildew Stain Remover (or equivalent) for tile and grout, or scrub tile with ammonia, and scrub grout with scouring powder. Wash with a bleach if needed. Rinse and dry.

Be sure to refer to the tile manufacturer's literature before cleaning or removing stains from resilient or hard tile. The manufacturer will make recommendations based on laboratory tests and customer comments. Some will even make specific product and brand name recommendations.

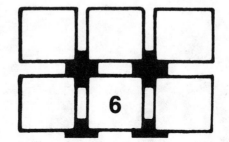

6

Repairing Tile Floors

Repairing resilient and hard tile floor coverings is actually much easier than most do-it-yourselfers realize. Defective tiles can easily be lifted and replaced with new tiles. In this chapter you'll learn how to make repairs to resilient and hard tile floors, as well as to the subflooring below them.

Hopefully, your floor doesn't look like that in Fig. 6-1. Even if it does, however, your flooring can be renewed or replaced. You should plan to execute all other interior repairs before beginning the repair of your floor. If you plan on saving the flooring material, cover it. Otherwise, ignore it as you make other repairs.

REPAIRING SELF-ADHERING TILE

There are numerous brands of self-adhering resilient tile on the market. The principles of installation and replacement are the same, however.

Once you've decided that a specific tile should be replaced, you should identify the problem and decide how many tiles will need replacement. Hopefully, you have some extra tiles in the garage

or up on a closet shelf for just such an emergency. By checking the unused tiles you can decide whether it is a self-adhering type or not.

When removing the old tile, be sure that you don't damage the adjacent tiles. One way of avoiding this is by cutting the defective tile in half and pulling it out from the center rather than the edges.

Once the defective self-adhering tile is removed, the subfloor should be checked for smoothness and possibly the reason why the tile is damaged. It may be that a subflooring nail has popped up or there was a rock or other object under the tile when it was laid. In any case, make sure that the replacement tile will not be damaged in the same manner.

With the defective tile removed and the area cleaned, lay the new tile into place with the adhesive cover still on. In this way, you can match the size and color of the tile and surrounding tiles before installation. Some linoleum and vinyl tiling will have faded in color. You may be able to use

Fig. 6-1. Hopefully, your floor doesn't look like this one (courtesy Azrock Floor Products).

Fig. 6-2. Installing replacement self-adhering tile.

common household bleach to match colors, or a thorough cleaning of the surrounding tile may rejuvenate the colors. Newer vinyl and better-quality no-wax flooring will probably not have faded and may only need a thorough cleaning (see Chapter 5).

Finally, strip off the backing paper and install the new self-adhering tile (Fig. 6-2). You may then want to place a heavy object, such as a block, on the surface to assist the bonding. Make sure that

the object will not mar the surface of the new tile. Depending upon the type of flooring, you may now want to wax or polish the floor, especially around the new tile.

REPAIRING RESILIENT TILE

The majority of resilient tile floors installed in new and older homes is not self-adhering, but is installed using a mastic or adhesive, as outlined in

Fig. 6-3. Tile floor with loose and damaged tile.

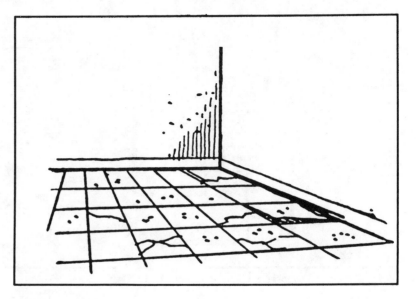

Chapter 3. So what do you do if tiles have come loose from the floor, are damaged, and need replacing (Fig. 6-3) and you want to do the job yourself?

First, you'll need some tools and supplies (Fig. 6-4). You'll need a container to mix in, tile adhesive for the kind of tile you have, a paint brush or putty knife, a knife or saw, and any new tile needed. If you don't have any leftover tile, check with the retailer from which you purchased the original tile. If you didn't install it, take a tile to any large tile retailer in the area for help on a match.

The first step to replacing resilient tile is to remove loose or damaged tile. A warm iron will help soften the adhesive (Fig. 6-5). Scrape off the old adhesive from the floor (Fig. 6-6). Also scrape the old adhesive from the back of the old tile if you are going to use it again.

Next, fit the tiles carefully. Some tile can be cut with a knife (Fig. 6-7) or shears; others with a saw. Tile is less apt to break if it is warm.

Spread the adhesive on the floor with a paint brush (Fig. 6-8) or putty knife, depending upon the consistency of the adhesive. Wait until the adhesive begins to set before placing the tile. Press the tile

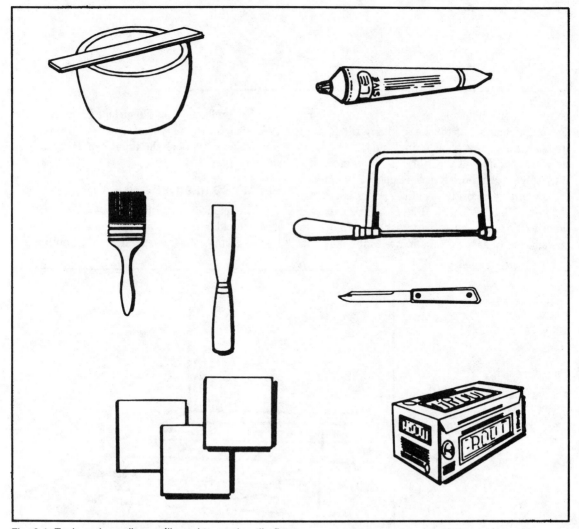

Fig. 6-4. Tools and supplies you'll need to repair a tile floor.

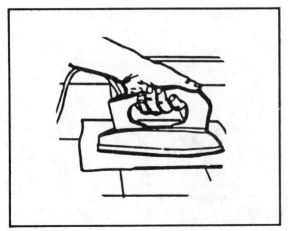

Fig. 6-5. Using a warm iron to soften the adhesive on the back of a floor tile.

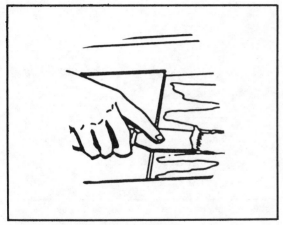

Fig. 6-6. Scrape off the old adhesive.

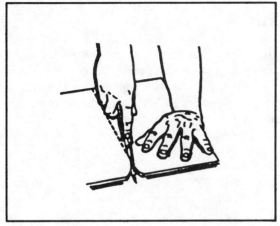

Fig. 6-7. Cut tile with a knife or household shears.

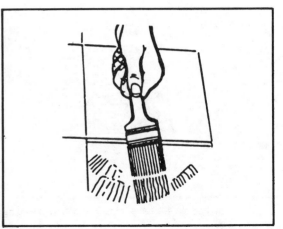

Fig. 6-8. Spread adhesive on the floor with a paint brush or putty knife.

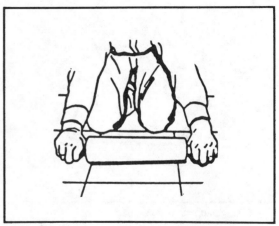

Fig. 6-9. Press the tile firmly with a rolling pin.

firmly into place and roll with a rolling pin (Fig. 6-9).

It's that easy. You've repaired your resilient tile floor and saved money, too.

REPAIRING CERAMIC TILE

The replacement or repair of ceramic tile is also easy to accomplish. The first step is to scrape off the old adhesive from the floor (Fig. 6-10). You can also scrape the adhesive from the old tile if you plan to reuse it.

If you are using new tile and need to fit it, mark it carefully to size. You can then score it with a tile cutter or a glass cutter. It will then snap off if you press it on the edge of a hard surface (Fig. 6-11).

163

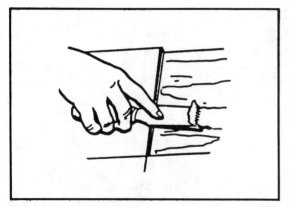

Fig. 6-10. Scrape old adhesive from floor before replacing ceramic tile.

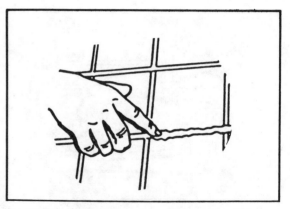

Fig. 6-13. Press the grout mixture between the tiles.

Fig. 6-11. Snapping a scored ceramic tile.

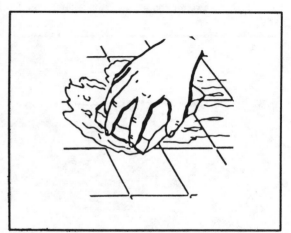

Fig. 6-14. Remove excess grout before it dries.

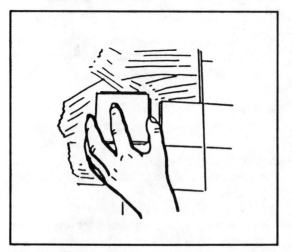

Fig. 6-12. Press the floor tile into place.

Spread the adhesive on the floor and on the back of the tile. Press the tile firmly into place (Fig. 6-12).

Joints on ceramic tile should be filled with grout after the tile has firmly set. Mix powdered grout with water to form a stiff paste. Then press the mixture into the joints with your fingers (Fig. 6-13). Smooth the surface. Carefully remove excess grout from the tile surface before it dries (Fig. 6-14).

Empty the excess grout mixture, disposing of it in a trash container—not down the drain. Then clean up surfaces and tools (Fig. 6-15). Allow the grout to dry before putting the floor back into use.

The job is complete and your ceramic tile floor is repaired. The same techniques can be used to repair ceramic wall tiles.

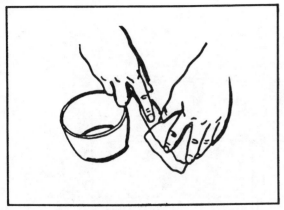

Fig. 6-15. Clean up tools and containers.

REPAIRING SUBFLOORS

The floors in most homes are composed of two separate layers. The bottom layer is called the subflooring and is made of rough, tongue-and-groove lumber nailed directly to the floor joists. In some cases the subflooring will run diagonally to the joists, while in others it will run at right angles to them. A layer of building paper often covers the subfloor to keep out dust and dirt. Then the finish flooring runs at right angles to the subfloor.

Here are a variety of maladies that occur in the subfloor and affect the finish flooring itself. One of the most common is the symptom of a creaking floor. In most cases, a creaking floor is caused by a loosening of the nails holding the subfloor to the joists. They may either pull loose or be loosened by shrinkage in the wood.

If the creak is in the subflooring and the underside is exposed, as when the flooring functions as the ceiling for an unfinished basement, drive a small wedge between the joist and the loose board (Fig. 6-16). It will take up the play in the board and the noise will stop. If several boards are loose, nail a piece of wood to the joist, high enough to prevent these boards from moving down (Fig. 6-17). The nailheads will keep the boards from moving up, effectively ending the noise.

In many cases, it is impossible to reach the subflooring without tearing up the finish floor or moving a ceiling. As neither of these is feasible, the only alternative is to try to locate the floor joist by tapping on the floor. If a floor joist near the creak is located, then 2-or 3-inch finishing nails can be driven through the subflooring and into the joist. Of course, this will require the removal of tiles in the area. The tiles can either be partially pulled back or replaced, as discussed earlier.

You may be required to repair a sagging subfloor before you install your tile floor. When this condition is found, it is generally because the floor joists and griders have been weakened by rot or by insects. In dealing with a weak and sagging floor, you will first have to raise it to its proper level. If it is the first floor with a basement underneath, the work can be done by a do-it-yourselfer. Use heavy lumber and a screw jack to accomplish the work (Fig. 6-18).

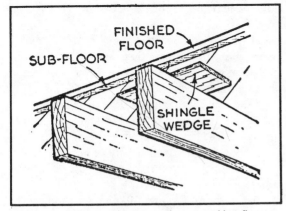

Fig. 6-16. Using a wedge to repair a squeaking floor.

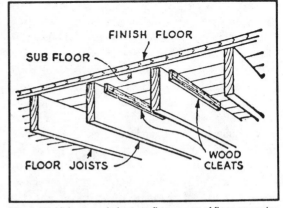

Fig. 6-17. Using wood cleats to fix a group of floor squeaks.

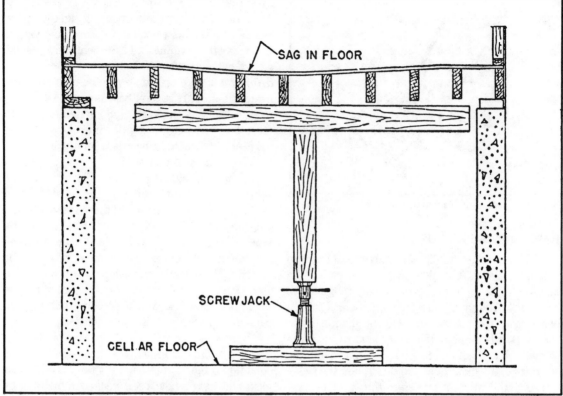

Fig. 6-18. Installing a screw jack to repair a sagging floor.

The size of the lumber should be about 4 × 4 inches. Place one of the timbers on the basement floor directly under the sag and put the screw jack on top of it. This beam will distribute the weight of the flooring over a relatively large portion of the basement flooring. If the basement flooring is of heavy concrete, this step won't be necessary.

Next, nail a piece of 4-×-4 along the sagging joists. Use a third piece of timber as a vertical beam from the top of the jack to the under portion of the 4-×-4 nailed to the joists. Turn up the jack until the floor is level. Don't attempt to bring the floor to a level position all at once. If this is done you may crack the walls and ceilings in the rooms above. Raise the jack only a fraction each week and you will avoid doing extensive damage to the house.

Check the position of the floor with a level and, when it is correct, measure the distance from the bottom of the horizontal 4-×-4 to the floor of the

basement. Cut a piece of 4-×-4 to this length. Turn the jack up enough to allow this beam to stand on end under the horizontal 4-×-4. Make sure that it is perfectly vertical and that it rests firmly on the floor. Remove the jack, along with the other timbers, leaving only one vertical and one horizontal 4-×-4.

If the entire floor is sagging, it will probably be necessary to use more than one vertical support. In this case, place a vertical 4-×-4 under each end of the horizontal beam.

When part of the total weight of a floor and the objects on it is supported by posts, it is important that each post have the proper footing. Most concrete floors in the basement are rather thin, and it is often necessary to prepare the floor before installing the posts.

To make a substantial footing for the posts in the basement floor, break up about 2 square feet of the concrete floor at the point where the post is to stand. Do this work with a heavy hammer or with a piece of pipe. Once the surface is broken, dig a hole about 12 inches deep and fill it with concrete made with 1 part cement, 2 parts sand, and 3 parts coarse aggregate. Level this with the floor, making a smooth surface, and allow about a week for the footing to dry before placing the posts upon it. Cover the concrete during this period and keep it moist.

Fortunately, most defects are associated with the first floor, and the basement underneath allows you to put in posts and other kinds of reinforcements. Sagging floors above the first floor level cannot practically be remedied, short of taking up the flooring and making extensive repairs.

PREVENTATIVE MAINTENANCE

The best way to make repairs to resilient and hard tile flooring is to prevent them by careful preparation, well-planned installation, and care of problems before they need to be repaired. Follow the suggestions in Chapter 5 on floor maintenance for the type of floor covering installed in your home.

You can also reduce repairs dramatically by shopping wisely for quality flooring products rather than purchasing the lowest-priced items. Purchase your flooring where you can also get valuable help and advice on the installation and care of your purchase. With the time and money you will be investing in your flooring, you want expert advice, not salesclerk guesses.

Another bit of advice offered by tile installers that has helped many do-it-yourselfers is to test first. Before you lay out your first floor, lay down a scrap piece of plywood and practice the installation. You can also begin your installation where the refrigerator will be installed or within a closet where any goofs will not be as evident.

The same practice is good advice for the first time you strip a floor or use special flooring preparations. Find somewhere out of the way to test the product or technique before using it on the main part of the flooring. Doing so will possibly save the replacement or repair of a portion of the flooring.

Finally, don't be ashamed of calling in expert advice if you have problems. Even if you didn't purchase the products at their store, most floor covering retailers will offer advice free of charge. They may not be familiar with the characteristics of the brands of tile and adhesive you purchased somewhere else, however. It's good economy to get quality advice from the people who sell you a quality product. The extra few dollars you may spend will be good insurance.

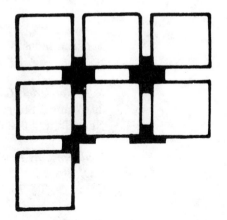

Suppliers

American Olean Tile Company, Inc.
P.O. Box 271
Lansdale, PA 19446
 Ceramic Mosaic Tile:
  103-113 So. Clark St.
  Olean, NY 14760
 Quarry Tile:
  Lewisport, KY 42351
 Quarry Tile:
  P.O. Box 1149
  Roseville, CA 95678

Armstrong World Industries
P.O. Box 3001
Lancaster, PA 17604

Aztec Ceramics Corporation
4735 Emil Road
San Antonio, TX 78219

Azrock Industries Inc.
P.O. Box 34030
San Antonio, TX 78233

Cambridge Tile Manufacturing Company
P.O. Box 15307
Cincinnati, OH 45215

Color Tile Supermart, Inc.
1400 Two Tandy Center
Fort Worth, TX 76101

Drakenfeld Colors/Ciba-Geigy Corp.
P.O. Box 519
Washington, PA 15301

Endicott Tile, Ltd.
P.O. Box 645
Fairbury, NB 68352

Ferro Corporation
1 Erieview Plaza
Cleveland, OH 44114

Florida Tile Division, Sikes Corp.
608 Prospect Street
Lakeland, FL 33802

Fusion Ceramics Inc.
P.O. Box 127
Carrollton, OH 44615

Gilmer Potteries, Inc.
P.O. Box 489
Gilmer, TX 75644

Hanley Brick Inc.
Administrative Office
Summerville, PA 15864-0068

O. Hommel Company
Hope Street
Carnegie, PA 15106

The Keller Corp.
3275 Penn Avenue
Hatfield, PA 19440

Lone Star Ceramics Company
P.O. Box 810215
Dallas, TX 75381

M & T Chemicals Inc.
P.O. Box 1104
Rahway, NJ 07065

Metropolitan Ceramics Inc.
P.O. Box 9240
Canton, OH 47711

Mid-State Tile Company
P.O. Box 1777
Lexington, NC 27292

Mid-State Tile Company
P.O. Box 734
Mount Gilead, NC 72306

New Castle Refractories Company
P.O. Box 471
New Castle, PA 16103

Niro Atomizer Inc.
9165 Rumsey Road
Columbia, MD 21045

Pemco Products, Inorganic Chemicals Div.
5601 Eastern Avenue
Baltimore, MD 21224

Quarry Tile Company
Spokane Industrial Park, Bldg. #12
Spokane, WA 99216

R.T. Vanderbilt Co., Inc.
30 Winfield Street
Norwalk, CT 06855

Southern Clay Products, Inc.
P.O. Box 44
Gonzales, TX 78629

Summitville Tiles Inc.
P.O. Box 73
Summitville, OH 43962

Swindell Dressler International Co.
441 Smithfield Street
Pittsburgh, PA 15222

TAM Ceramics, Inc.
Box C Bridge Station
Niagara Falls, NY 14305

Terra Designs Inc.
211 Jockey Hollow Road
Bernardsville, NJ 07924

Tile Council of America, Inc.
P.O. Box 326
Princeton, NJ 08542

Universal Ceramics, Inc.
P.O. Box 483
Adairsville, GA 30103

Wenczel Tile Company
P.O. Box 5308
Trenton, NJ 08638

Wenczel Tile Company of Florida
P.O. Box 19368
Tampa, FL 33616

The Willette Corporation
P.O. Box 28
New Brunswick, NJ 08903

Winburn Tile Manufacturing Company
P.O. Box 1369
Little Rock, AR 72203

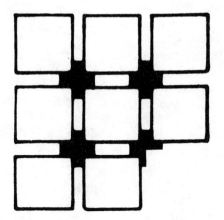

Glossary

asphalt emulsion—A natural bituminous product, similar to tar, which is used as a waterproofing medium.

backing—Any material used as a base, or crude framework, over which a finish material is to be applied. It is usually lumber, such as between studding to provide a more solid area over which metal lath can be nailed. Also refers to boards used as nailing bearing where studs or joists have been omitted.

beating in—The process of moving a small board over the tile, while striking it lightly with a hammer, to set the tile firmly into the mortar and in one smooth plane.

bisque—The body of the tile, made of some type of clay, and excluding the glaze. Sometimes called the *biscuit.*

bond—Refers to adherence of one material to another, as of coats of mortar, tile to mortar, brick to mortar, etc. Also used to designate the patterns in which brick are laid, as common bond, Flemish bond, etc., which indicates the arrangement or overlapping of bricks or stones to tie the wall together.

bush hammer—A hammer having a rectangular head and two corrugated or toothed faces; used for roughing concrete to provide a masonry bond.

buttering—Coating the tile, also the mortar, with a mixture of pure cement and water to hold the tile in place and to make a bond between the tile and the mortar.

caulking—Refers to the filling in of joints or crevices with a type of mastic or by tamping in oakum or other wadding.

caulking compound—Originally a product made by saturating oakum with asphalt or tar and used for filling cracks, as in ships. Now the term refers to any puttylike compound that is waterproof and is used for filling cracks around windows, etc. Many modern types are known as *mastic.*

cement—A product of certain types of limestone, containing lime, silica, and alumina, some kinds of which must be roasted and then pulverized. It has the property of hardening under water and is used in many types of mortar to bond sand together. When set, it is very hard.

ceramic—An article made of baked clay. In the tile trade, the word is used to designate a tile made of compressed clay and silica, which is rather glassy or vitreous in nature and will not absorb water.

chase—A type of construction that makes use of the rabbet principle. Glass blocks are commonly set into such a channel to lock them in place at the edges of panels.

chipping off—Cutting away mortar or concrete with a sharp-edged tool such as a hammer or chisel.

crystal—A rather rough, transparent glaze which has greater depth than ordinary glazes and imparts a design effect to the tile.

dutchman—A path made on a wood surface as a repair when too much wood has been taken away or when an unnecessary cutout has been made.

efflorescence—A white powder, actually fine crystals, of the soluble salts contained in mortar, that appears on concrete after it has set for a few days. Often referred to as *alkali*.

encaustic—Refers to etching clay tiles and filling in or inlaying with another color of clay. After smoothing, the tiles are baked to harden them.

etched—Cut into the face or engraved.

expansion strips—Strips of cork or sometimes soft fiber sheets, saturated with asphalt or other waterproofing. Used at the edges of glass panels or concrete to provide room for expansion when they become warm.

fresno—A large cement finisher's trowel fitted with a long wood handle, like a hoe, and having a pivot arrangement. It permits troweling of large areas without the need to walk on the concrete surface.

furring—Stripping used to build out a surface, such as a studded wall, where strips of suitable size are added to the studs to accommodate vent pipes or other fixtures.

gauging—Providing strips set at a desirable distance from the wall being tiled as a guide to maintain a required thickness of mortar.

glaze—Melted silica, or sand, which coats the tile body, or bisque, giving it a transparent glassy finish. It is somewhat harder than ordinary glass.

gloss—A bright or shiny finish that reflects light much like glass. Also the luster of a polished surface.

hydraulic—Denotes a force exerted by water, as the setting of cement through the action of water combining to form a catalyst.

lacquer—A varnishlike product made from the resinous substance obtained from the lac insect of India. It is mixed with an ethyl alcohol.

lath—A wood strip or metal mesh that receives the plaster and acts as a background or reinforcing agent for the plaster.

masonite—A trade name for a type of fiberboard made of cane fiber and pressed under great pressure to form a thin, hard sheet.

mastic—A name applied to various sticky or sometimes puttylike substances, which are made of true resins, with whiting, asbestos, or other materials added. It never hardens completely; its pliability makes it useful for many purposes, including the setting of tile.

matte—A semirough glaze; makes a surface similar to an eggshell.

mold—To form a pliable substance into some desired shape. Generally done by pressing the material into a form or box provided for the purpose.

monolith—Refer to a pillar or column of a single stone. When concrete is poured to form such a pillar, it is referred to as monolithic pouring, since it is all of one aggregate. This would not be true if concrete were poured over large stones.

mortar—A combination of sand, cement, either fireclay or lime, and water, often used in the installation of hard tiles.

mosaic—Small bits of tile, stone, glass, etc., that form a surface design of intricate pattern. Often laid over mortar or metal.

mural—A sort of picture done with small pieces of tile and intended for use on a wall as a decorative effect.

oakum—Jute or hemp fibers loosely twisted together and saturated with asphalt or other tarlike material. Used for caulking.

patio—A courtyard or inner court. A Spanish word that has come to be used in America to designate a partly enclosed porch; hence the tile used on such a floor is known as patio tile.

patty tile—A corruption of the word patio, referring to large clay tile used for patio floors.

patty trowel—A term used to describe a trowel intermediate in size between a pointer and a mason's trowel. Used for packing damp mortar.

pier—Usually a short built-up or cast column that is free standing; that is, not joined to other work and designed to support horizontal beams, such as floor stringers.

plastic—A pliable substance capable of being molded or formed.

pointing—Filling in joints with mortar or repairing holes. See *tuck pointing*.

quarry—Used to designate tiles that are large and thick, similar to slabs of stone cut in a quarry. These are vitreous tiles and require no soaking.

refractories—Clays or claylike products that do not fuse or melt readily. They are suitable for tile bisques since as they will not melt when the glaze is baked over the surface.

relief—Part of a design that projects beyond the plane for face of a molded or sculptured design.

riser—The upright portion of a stair step that supports the front of the tread. The part that keeps the toe from getting under the tread.

satin matte—A glaze intermediate between high gloss and common matte that imparts a silky sheen to the tile.

scarifier—A piece of thin sheet metal with teeth or serrations cut in the edge like a saw blade and used to roughen mortar surfaces to provide a good bond. Also known as a *scratcher*.

screed—A strip of wood, often 2 × 4 inches, set down as a guide for attaining a level surface of concrete. In the tile trade, it refers to a piece of wood used as a straightedge.

silica—A naturally quartz occurring as clear crystals or as sand with various other minerals in mixture,

silicon—The chief constituent of sand or glass, it is nonmetallic and, when melted, is more or less transparent and glassy. A form of quartz.

stretcher—A term used to designate the individual pieces of tile trim with the exception of in or out angles. The latter are always known by their regular names, such as "in angles," "out angles," "up angles," or "down angles."

tapping in—Tapping in tile lightly with the handle of the pointer as a preliminary means of setting them into place.

terra-cotta—A composition of clay and fine sand, either red or yellowish in color, used in making tile bisquies, hollow tile, or flue linings.

terrazzo—A type of floor or wall finish obtained by embedding small-sized pebbles or crushed rock in concrete and grinding and polishing the surface to a smooth finish.

texture—Used in speaking of the type of glaze or finish used in tiles. The texture may be high glass, matter, or somewhat etched.

tuck pointing—Filling in crevices, as with mortar, mastic, etc.

unglazed—Without a glaze; refers to pressed and baked tiles with a smooth, earthy surface.

vitreous—Glassy in texture and containing sand that has been melted. Vitreous tiles will not absorb water.

Index

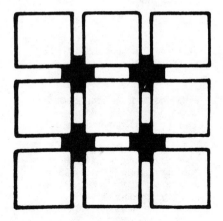

Index

OTHER POPULAR TAB BOOKS OF INTEREST